ON THE ROAD IN EUROPE

Transfăgărășan, Romania
45°36'19.5"N 24°37'03.0"E

The signposting for hikers is well organised in Romania's beautiful Ceahlău Mountains.

Piciorul Verdele
Polana Țiflic
Izvorul Alb
Bâtca Cerebuc
1156 m
P.Izvorul Alb
Chica Balcului
Secu
Obcina Horștei
1062 m
Curmătura La Morminte
Căciula Dorobanțului
Piatra Lată
Stânca Dochiei
Panaghia
Cab.Izvorul Muntelui
797 m
Izvorul Muntelui
Vf. TOACA
1904 m
Vf. Lespezi
1802 m
Piatra cu Apa
Curmătura Lutu Roșu 1020 m
P.Izvorul Muntelui
Polana Popii
Cab.Dochia
1750 m
Bâtca lui Ghedeon
1845 m
Vf.Ocolașul Mare
1907 m
Obcina Piatra Arsă
Vf. Piatra Sură

Molden, Norway
61°20'17.1"N 7°18'09.4"E

Saarschleife, Orscholz, Germany
49°30'06.9"N 6°32'27.2"E

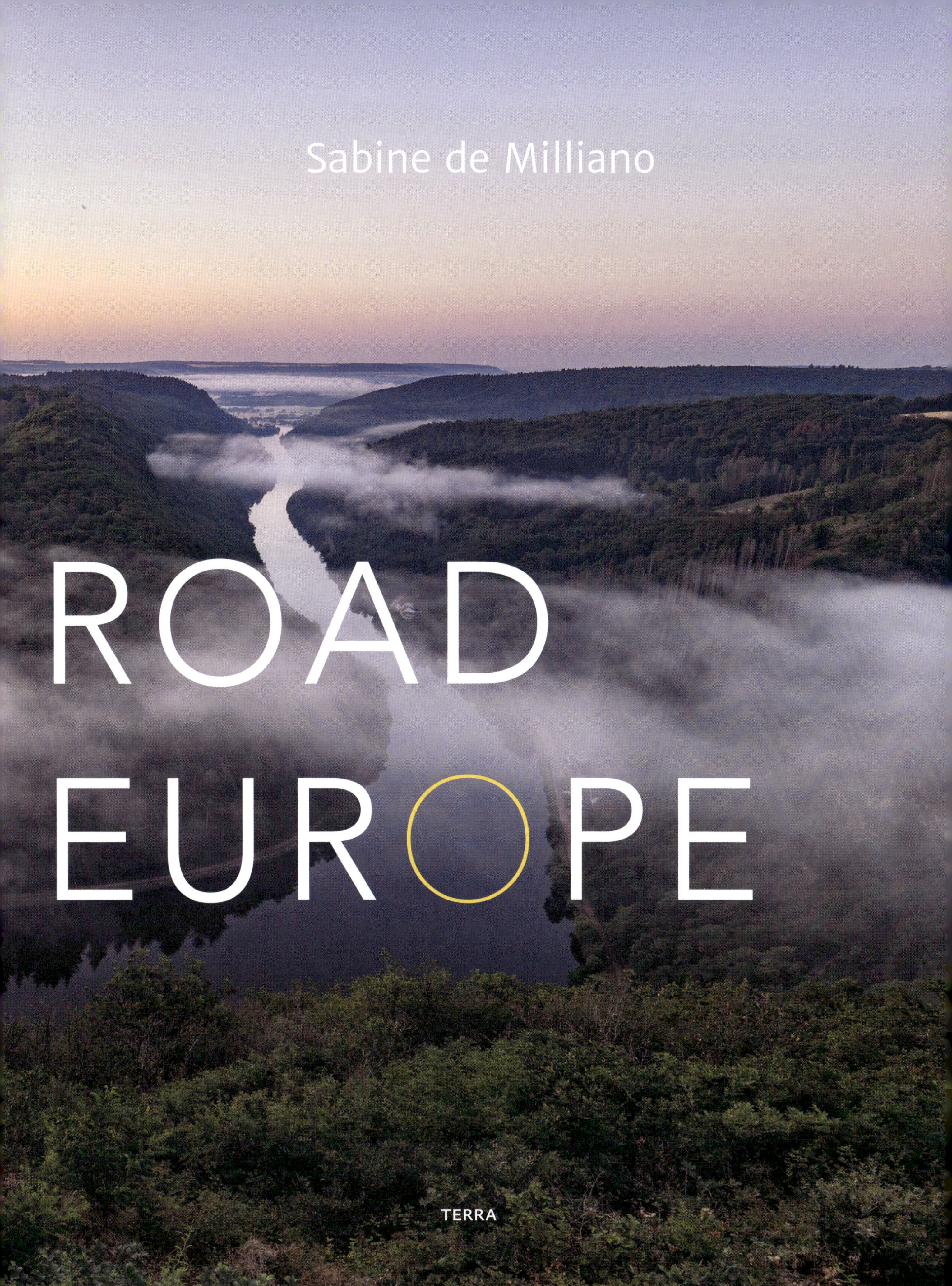

Sabine de Milliano
ROAD
EUROPE
TERRA

5
2
3
1
6
4

Contents

Introduction

Happiness is found in the little things – and in being on the road in Europe. A gorgeous viewpoint just around the corner, a friendly encounter with locals or fellow travellers, a delicious meal after a long hike in nature, or spotting wildlife right in front of you. I remember countless moments when I was pleasantly surprised while being on the road. Over the past 15 years, I have travelled more than 150,000 kilometres through over 50 countries, including all European nations. The greatest lesson that I have learned on all those adventures is that you do not have to travel far to see and experience beautiful things. Europe has it all and offers enough for a lifetime of travelling!

No other continent has such a large diversity in nature and culture in a small geographic area as Europe does. That makes it perfect for an adventure on the road. Starting your journey from your front door – or an airport if you are coming from another continent after reading this book – means that you will gradually progress to your farthest destination. Along the way, you will notice changes in climate, architecture, trees, language, food, culture, wildlife, and much more. Some changes are gradual, while others are abrupt. By driving through Europe instead of flying, you will experience the diversity of our planet's ecosystem and learn the geopolitical history of Europe in a way that no schoolbook can ever teach you. A road trip is simply an unforgettable, fulfilling, and thought-provoking adventure that I would recommend to anyone. Through this book, I hope to inspire others to hit the road and appreciate it as much as I do.

This book describes six road trips through 25 countries. All of them are suitable for travelling by car, camper, caravan, or motorcycle, and various types of accommodations are available along the routes to spend the night. Some countries are also excellent destinations for wild camping, for those who love to fully immerse themselves in nature.

'A road trip is simply an unforgettable, fulfilling, and thought-provoking adventure that I would recommend to anyone'

The six road trips vary in length and level of adventure, but none of them require specific skills or extensive preparation. They are accessible to anyone who is open to driving in unknown terrain and exploring what lies beyond the horizon. The road trips will take you past some of Europe's most stunning landscapes, picturesque towns, and vibrant cultures that will leave a lasting impression on you. Most of my personal favourites are included, although I should point out that it is impossible to cover all of Europe's diversity and splendour in one book of 256 pages. But if you ever come to the point where you have completed all the trips of this book, I am confident that you will have the experience and curiosity to discover the other geographic regions of this fantastic continent as well. Let these pages mark the beginning of many new road trip adventures for you.

Enjoy the journey!

Camping out in the wild in Laponia, Sweden's northern wilderness.

Făgăraș Mountains, Romania
45°36'29.4"N 24°37'02.1"E

1

PEAKS OF THE EAST

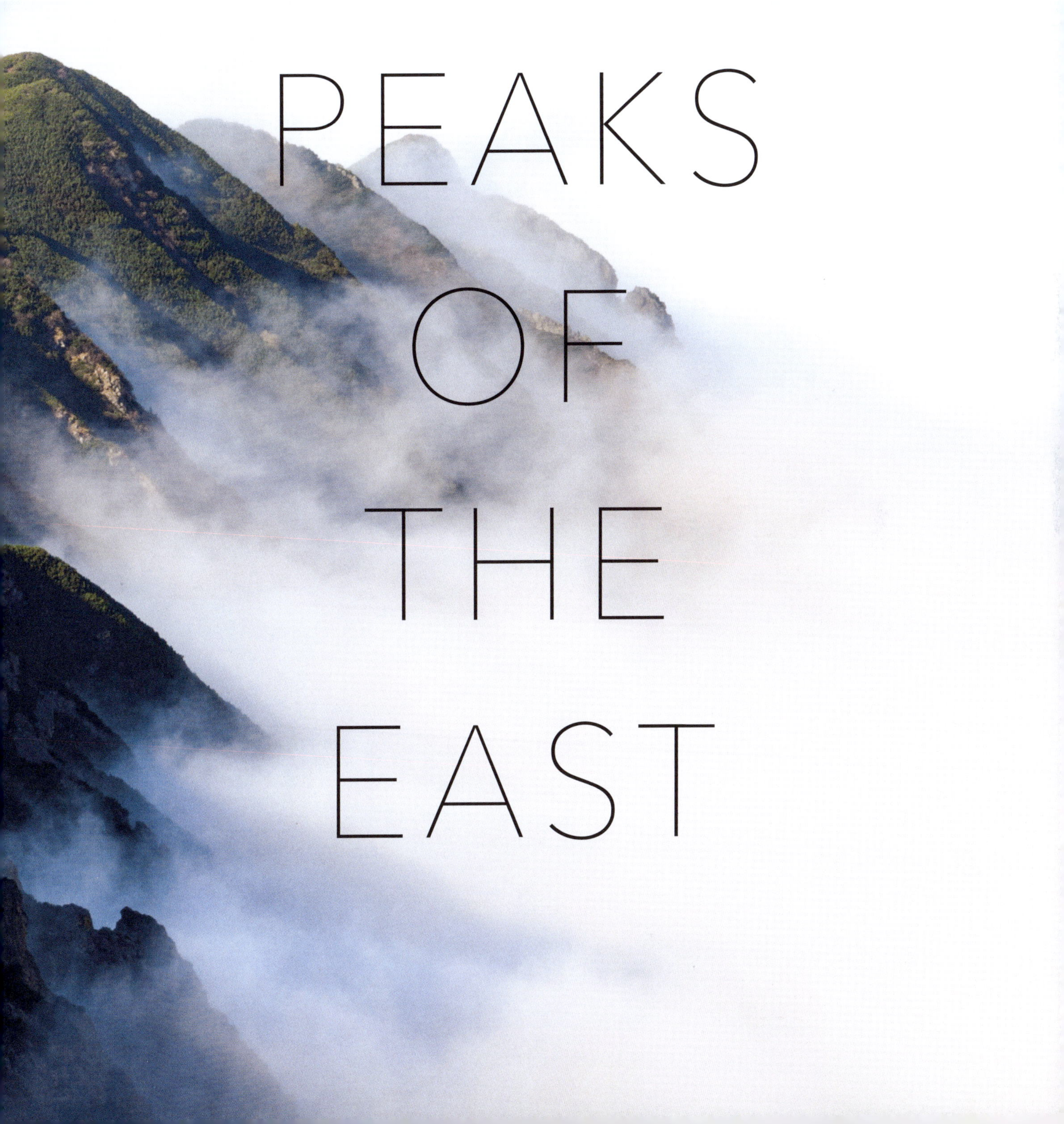

An adventurous journey through **the Carpathians**

Thousands of peaks, hundreds of villages and dozens of photogenic cities colour the journey through the Carpathian Mountains. Although this is a relatively unknown part of Europe for many, this geographic region is a true delight for road trip travellers. Offering a balanced mixture of adventure, fabulous scenery, culture, and hospitality, Eastern Europe will undoubtedly steal your heart.

Hike through ancient forests and admire the views from the summits of unspoiled mountain ranges. Stroll through inviting cities and towns while enjoying some of the best historical architecture where you least expect it. Taste the local flavours – the countries of the Carpathians offer an interesting cuisine influenced by many cultures – and try some of the best wines from our continent. Last but not least, be sure to drive the Transfăgărășan, one of the best and most impressive roads in the world!

When you go exploring the East, you should visit Romania in particular. This is one of my favourite destinations in Europe and a country full of pleasant surprises and friendly encounters. Weather permitting, life happens out on the street, and it is a joy to observe the street scene while driving through towns and villages. Outside of the residential areas, there is a range of natural landscapes waiting to be discovered. Whether you will go left or right at the next crossroad, you will not be disappointed.

GERMANY

CZECH REPUBLIC

POLAND

SLOVAKIA

HUNGARY

ROMANIA

My dog Alex in Tiské stěny, Czech Republic
50°47'11.9"N 14°01'46.9"E

THE COMPLETE ROUTE

An adventurous journey through **the Carpathians**

Total length
2900 km

Countries
Germany | Czech Republic | Poland
Slovakia | Hungary | Romania

Time
3-4 weeks

Best season
May to early June and late August to October. Summers are hot, winters can be harsh. Beware that some mountain roads such as Transfăgărășan (DN7C) are open only for a few months each year. Bohemian Switzerland can be visited in winter as well.

Destinations
1 **Dresden**
2 **Bohemian Switzerland** – 60 km
3 **Kraków** – 510 km
4 **High Tatras** – 190 km
5 **Banská Štiavnica** – 160 km
6 **Tokaj** – 240 km
7 **Maramureș** – 310 km
8 **Ceahlău** – 230 km
9 **Sighișoara** – 190 km
10 **Bucegi Mountains** – 170 km
11 **Transfăgărășan** – 220 km
12 **Sibiu** – 80 km
13 **Retezat** – 170 km
14 **Apuseni** – 220 km
15 **Cluj-Napoca** – 150 km

Balance*
Nature ●●●●
Culture ●●●●●
Culinary ●●●

* (max 5 dots)

SHORTER ROUTES

Colours and flavours of **Eastern Europe**

Total length
1050 km

Time
2 weeks

Destinations
5 | 6 | 7 | 9 | 12 | 15

Balance
Nature ●●
Culture ●●●●●
Culinary ●●●

Highlights of **Transylvania**

Total length
1100 km

Time
2-3 weeks

Destinations
7 | 8 | 9 | 10 | 11 | 12 | 15

Balance
Nature ●●●●
Culture ●●●●
Culinary ●●●

From **Summit** to **Summit**

Total length
1600 km

Time
3 weeks

Destinations
4 | 7 | 8 | 10 | 11 | 13

Balance
Nature ●●●●
Culture ●●●
Culinary ●●

GERMANY
CZECH REPUBLIC
SLOVAKIA
HUNGARY
ROMANIA
1
2
3
4
5
6
7
8
9
10
11
12
13
14
15

GERMANY

1 Dresden

This road trip adventure starts in Dresden, the charming capital of the German state of Saxony. The detailed façades colouring the heart of the city make you feel like you are strolling through an historical old town. But do not judge a book by its cover – the city was almost entirely rebuilt in its original style after being largely destroyed during World War II. This does not change the historical atmosphere of the *Altstadt*, though, and you will appreciate how they have been able to rebuild this photogenic city.

Dresden, Germany
51°03'18.8"N 13°44'28.6"E

CZECH REPUBLIC

2 Bohemian Switzerland

The landscape of České Švýcarsko, as this nature park is officially known, is a unique mix of sandstone sculptures and dense forests. You can spend hours hiking here while enjoying the views from the many peaks, hills and rock formations that characterise the area. Regardless of the season or weather, spending a few days in this region is a great stop on your journey to the Carpathian Mountains. My favourite location in the park is the forest of Tiské stěny (Tisa Rocks). With its impressive natural sandstone statues, it is a perfect destination for what I enjoy most: hiking and photography.

EXPLORE

Bohemian Switzerland is also known for its colourful glass art. There are several studios and workshops within an hour's drive of Bohemian Switzerland, such as Novotný in Nový Bor and Ajeto in Lindava. At both locations, you can enjoy a cup of coffee while watching glass objects being made live right in front of you.

Sněžná, Krásná Lípa, Czech Republic
50°55'26.6"N 14°28'56.6"E

Sněžník, Czech Republic
50°48'22.8"N 14°06'15.9"E

The Cloth Hall, Kraków, Poland
50°03'43.9"N 19°56'15.2"E

510 km

POLAND

3 Kraków

Kraków has a rich history and is a bustling cultural city, of which Rynek Główny (the Main Market Square) is the beating heart. With a size of roughly 40,000 m^2, this is the largest medieval market square in Europe. Kraków's university also originates from the medieval era, and the many students in the city contribute to the positive vibe and trendy food scene.

EXPLORE

Make a stop at Szklarska Poręba on the edge of the Giant Mountains (*Krkonoše*), which is a popular base for hiking, mountain biking, and skiing. Visit the Kamieńczyk waterfall or take a walk to the top of Szrenica mountain if you have more time.

Rynek Główny, Kraków, Poland
50°03'44.4"N 19°56'13.6"E

190 km

SLOVAKIA

4 High Tatras

EXPLORE

Less than an hour's drive from Štrbské Pleso lie the imposing ruins of Spiš Castle, one of the largest castles in Europe and worth a visit just for its size.

Sharing the border of Poland and Slovakia, the High Tatras form the highest part of the Carpathian Mountains with about ten peaks exceeding 2600 metres. Outdoor and mountain sports enthusiasts can spend weeks here. If you have time and love mountain hiking, I recommend climbing Kriváň, praised by many as the most beautiful mountain in Slovakia. Or experience the mountain atmosphere at lower elevations and take a shorter hike from the village of Štrbské Pleso, located by the scenic lake of the same name.

The High Tatras in the distance – the highest summits of the Carpathian Mountains.

160 km

SLOVAKIA

5 Banská Štiavnica

The rough peaks of the Carpathians slowly give way to flower meadows and picturesque towns as you travel further south. One of them is the romantic Banská Štiavnica, which offers opportunities for photography both day and night. The historic city centre, with about 10,000 inhabitants, was declared a UNESCO World Heritage Site in 1993. Despite this status and its past as an attractive place for gold and silver mining, mass tourism has not yet taken hold in Banská Štiavnica. Let us just hope it will stay that way.

Banská Štiavnica, Slovakia
48°27'25.2"N 18°54'13.3"E

HUNGARY

6 Tokaj

Wine lovers undoubtedly know the name and reputation of the famous Tokaj wine, the sweet wine made from white grapes that, after so-called *noble rot*, give a strong aroma and pronounced taste. The stronger the sweetness, the higher the score of *Puttonyos* – in the wine trade, you can find them between 3 and 6. Whether you like wine or not, a tasting session of these strange but tasty wines is an intriguing experience, especially when it takes place in one of the many underground cellars.

Cellar entrance, Tolcsva, Tokaj, Hungary
48°16'53.1"N 21°27'26.1"E

ROMANIA

7 Maramureș

Romania is the heart of the Carpathian Mountains and for most travellers the most spectacular part of the journey. One of the first highlights after crossing the border (which usually goes quick and without problems) is the rural landscape of Maramureș. Here, time seems to stand still. Enjoy the relaxed atmosphere, historic wooden churches, and local cheeses while imagining yourself in the era before the modern car – horse and carriage as the primary means of transportation is still common here.

EXPLORE

Visit the brightly decorated tombstones of the *Merry Cemetery* in Săpânța, the most cheerful cemetery you will probably ever visit. Less cheerful but imposing is a visit to Sighet Prison in Sighetu Marmației, which provides a fascinating insight into Romania's communist era.

Horse-drawn carts are still commonly seen in the Romanian countryside, especially in the northern regions.

EXPLORE

The monastery complex of Bârsana is a must-see along the way, with its iconic wooden churches and romantic gardens.

The village of Vişeu de Sus is an attractive base with a wide choice of accommodation. From here, you can also explore the mountains in the Maramureş Mountains Natural Park or the Rodna Mountains National Park.

A summer day in the gardens of Bârsana.

Bârsana Monastery, Romania
47°47'33.7"N 24°05'30.3"E

ROMANIA

8 Ceahlău

EXPLORE

Neamț Monastery is not only an active religious community but also a testament to the cultural and artistic heritage of Romania, since it is one of the oldest religious settlements in the country.

On your way to the Ceahlău Mountains, you can make a detour to visit the painted monasteries of Bukovina, such as the colourful Voroneț near Gura Humorului.

Romania has several mountain ranges that are no less impressive in terms of natural beauty than the much more famous Alps. One of my favourites are the Ceahlău Mountains. Numerous pointed rock formations decorate the landscape here, while vast forests without any visible signs of civilization make you wonder where Romania's 19 million people are living. Ceahlău's well-marked hiking trails lead to excellent viewpoints where you can enjoy the rugged landscapes of Eastern Europe. Also, keep an eye on the ground for bear tracks because one of Europe's largest populations of brown bears lives here.

View from Vârful Toaca, Ceahlău Mountains, Romania
46°58'38.9"N 25°56'59.7"E

Monk Gregory at Neamț Monastery, Romania.

With sore muscles after a long day of hiking in the Ceahlău Massif, we take a break from the mountains and visit Neamț Monastery, one of the oldest monasteries of Romania. Monk Gregory starts a chat with me, who – to my big surprise – seems to know everything about Dutch football teams and the monarchy of the Netherlands. A former mathematician, Gregory is a walking encyclopaedia and a good laugh at the same time. He wants to take a photo together and asks if I am willing to email the photo, after which he immediately asks: 'You have email in the Netherlands, right?'

Sighișoara, Romania
46°13'08.3"N 24°47'32.4"E

190 km

ROMANIA

9 Sighișoara

Sighișoara is nestled in the heart of Transylvania. The town is dominated by a 12th-century hilltop citadel, featuring a clock tower and colourful houses that surround it. Sighișoara has a friendly and relaxed medieval atmosphere, which is best experienced by simply wandering through the narrow cobblestone streets or by enjoying a coffee in one of the cosy cafés. Its colourful houses and romantic vistas make it one my favourite photographic locations in Romania.

EXPLORE

Sighișoara is the supposed birthplace of Vlad Dracula, the inspiration behind Bram Stoker's Dracula. In this part of Romania, you will see more merchandise and tourism focused on Dracula, but you will also learn that the real story of Vlad is quite different from that of Dracula.

Sighișoara, Romania
46°13'11.5"N 24°47'33.7"E

170 km

ROMANIA

10 Bucegi Mountains

EXPLORE

The nearby Sinaia is one of the oldest and most famous mountain resorts of Romania. Its half-timbered jewels like Peleș Castle and Sinaia Monastery are a visual contrast to the wild mountains surrounding it.

Bucegi Natural Park is characterised by a large mountain plateau that is covered by intriguing rock sculptures. A ride in a *telecabina* or *telegondola* from Sinaia takes you to the top of the Bucegi mountain plateau, from where you can enjoy a hike over the mountain ridges. With wide views above the tree line, you feel like you are walking on the roof of Europe.

Bușteni, Romania
45°24'25.9"N 25°31'46.6"E

Durău, Romania
47°00'06.9"N 25°54'49.4"E

220 km

ROMANIA

11 Transfăgărășan

Marked by some as the best road in the world, the Transfăgărășan is a destination on its own. Despite its brutal and controversial construction during the rule of Romania's dictator Nicolae Ceaușescu, nowadays this mountain road is loved by many. The Transfăgărășan is crawling through the landscape like a serpentine with the peaks of Romania's wildest mountains on both sides. Do not be surprised to find supercars here, or old-timers and whatever else with two or four wheels: those who like to drive and love awe-inspiring landscapes will find their way here. Beware that this road is only open for a few months a year, though – winters are harsh here.

EXPLORE

Close to the highest point of the Transfăgărășan you will find Cascada Capra, a scenic waterfall just next to the road.

The eye-catching Bâlea Lac on the mountain pass is a glacier lake that is absolutely worth a stroll to. From the top of the mountain pass you can also start one of the many hiking trails in the wild Făgăraș Mountains.

Cascada Capra, Romania
45°35'10.4"N 24°37'50.9"E

Transfăgărășan, Romania
45°35'08.1"N 24°37'34.3"E

‘Marked by some as the best road in the world, the Transfăgărășan is a destination on its own’

Bâlea Lac, Romania
45°36’14.6”N 24°36’56.9”E

ROMANIA

12 Sibiu

The gorgeous Transfăgărășan ends near Sibiu, which is gorgeous in its own way. This fortified medieval town in Transylvania became a Saxon town called *Hermannstadt* in the 12th century. Although many of the ethnic Germans moved to Germany and Austria after World War II, some decided to stay in Sibiu. The German atmosphere is still present today and makes Sibiu an interesting cultural destination.

Sibiu, Romania
45°47'55.4"N 24°09'01.7"E

Stray dog Negru leads the way in the pristine Retezat Mountains.

In 2013, I made an unforgettable hike through the Retezat Mountains with a special guide: a stray dog named Negru led the way during an 8-hour trek through the forest, over steep rocks, and even through snow. In places where the markings had been erased by the elements of nature, he pointed out the right path with confidence. I shared my water supply with him because it was warm that day in June and I was afraid that my new friend would dehydrate in the burning sun. And though this meant that I would not reach the summit due to insufficient water reserves, Negru made this hiking trip truly unforgettable.

170 km

ROMANIA

13 Retezat

Towards the end of the 1500-kilometres-long Carpathian Mountains, you will arrive in the tranquil Retezat Mountains. Here you can enjoy hiking through rugged, untouched nature. Retezat is characterised by its rugged peaks, deep valleys, and glacial lakes – there are more than 80 of them! Hikers are drawn to Retezat for its extensive network of trails, offering opportunities for various skill levels to enjoy the dense forests and alpine landscapes of the Southern Carpathian Mountains.

EXPLORE

Natural geological monument Râpa Roșie (*red ravine*) is a landscape of bare red rocky pillars. They are formed by erosion and runoff, which has led to a peculiar badlands landscape.

Near Vârful Retezat, Romania
45°23'03.2"N 22°51'03.7"E

220 km

ROMANIA

14 Apuseni

The last mountain range of the Carpathians in this road trip is Apuseni in western Romania. Here, not only the mountains are photogenic, but also the underground world. The nearby Meziad Cave – known in Romanian as Peștera Meziad – is an underground hidden gem. You will not find disco lights and music for decoration here, but pure silence and only some simple lights to help you experience the size of this theatre below the Earth's surface.

Peștera Meziad, Romania
46°45'46.1"N 22°28'43.6"E

ROMANIA

15 Cluj-Napoca

Cluj-Napoca is one of the largest cities in Romania, yet a city with a relaxed atmosphere. It has played an important role in the history of Transylvania and is therefore still considered the (unofficial) capital of the region today. *Cluj*, as the city is called colloquially, is also home to the largest university in the country. Full of culture, history, and culinary spots, Cluj-Napoca is a great endpoint of our journey through the Carpathians, where you can let all the impressions of this part of Europe sink in quietly while enjoying a good glass of Romanian wine made from Fetească neagră, my favourite indigenous grape variety.

EXPLORE

If you want to end your journey through the Carpathians with an obscure but thrilling day out, then visit the underground Salina Turda, an enormous salt mine of which a part is turned into a subsurface amusement park.

Cluj-Napoca, Romania
46°46'25.2"N 23°34'56.2"E

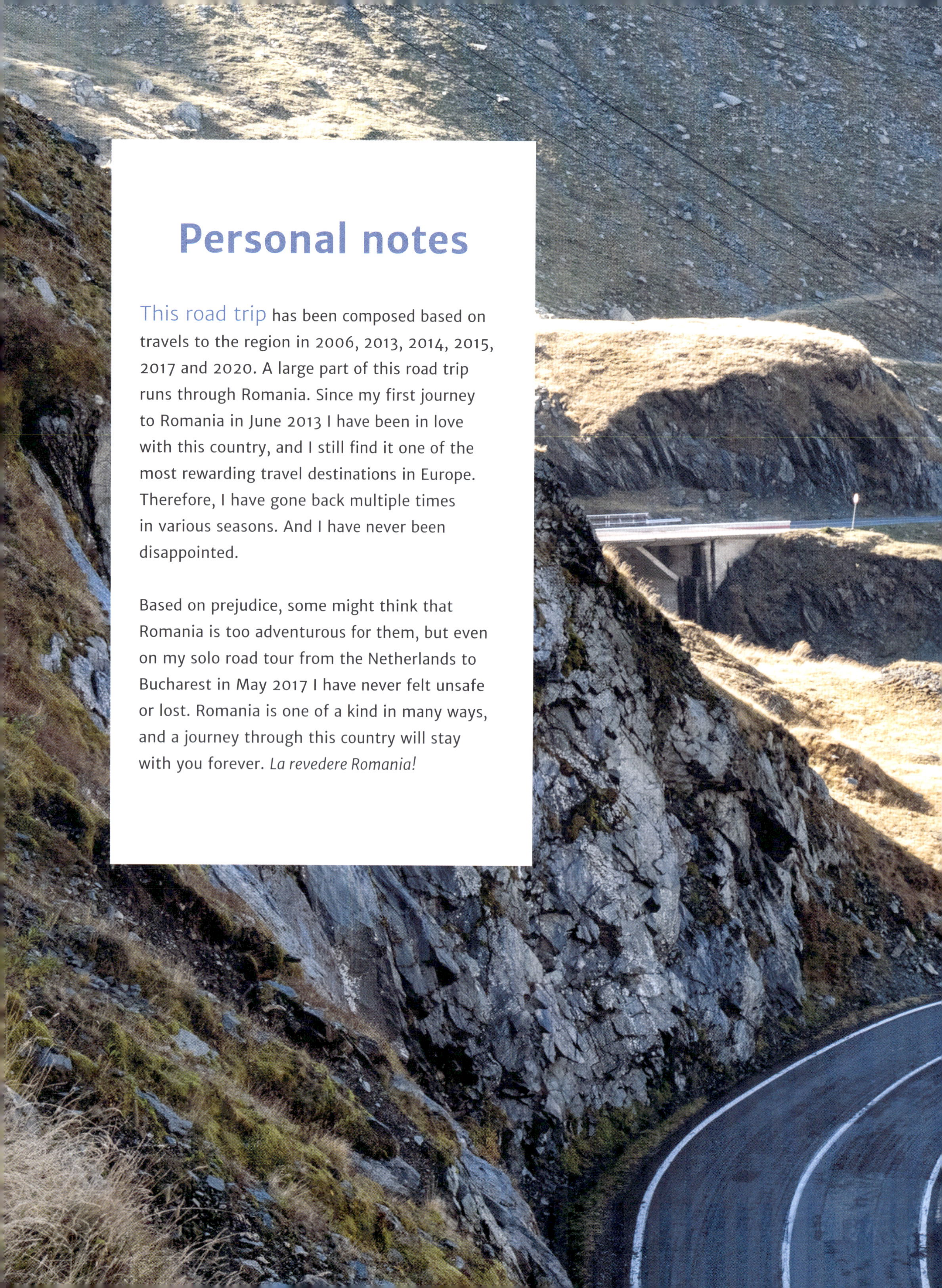

Personal notes

This road trip has been composed based on travels to the region in 2006, 2013, 2014, 2015, 2017 and 2020. A large part of this road trip runs through Romania. Since my first journey to Romania in June 2013 I have been in love with this country, and I still find it one of the most rewarding travel destinations in Europe. Therefore, I have gone back multiple times in various seasons. And I have never been disappointed.

Based on prejudice, some might think that Romania is too adventurous for them, but even on my solo road tour from the Netherlands to Bucharest in May 2017 I have never felt unsafe or lost. Romania is one of a kind in many ways, and a journey through this country will stay with you forever. *La revedere Romania!*

Transfăgărășan, Romania
45°36'19.5"N 24°37'03.0"E

Must-have items
for your road trip

Apart from your passport, payment cards, phone, and toothbrush, there are a few things that are very handy to take with you on your road trip. Here comes a list of the additional items that I find essential. They can be of great help on your own road adventure!

PAPER MAPS

Apps on your phone or laptop are handy to use for navigation, but nothing beats a paper map for travel planning. More so, studying a paper map of the region you are in or heading off to will increase your knowledge and appreciation of the area.

MOTOR OIL

On any road trip it is a good habit to check your car's motor oil level once every 1000-2000 kilometres. Bring along one or two litres of motor oil to replenish your car's juices whenever it is needed. You can best check it in the morning before you start the engine for the first time of the day.

FIRELIGHTERS & A GOOD LIGHTER

While I want to limit the endorsement of brands in this book, I will make an exception here: the PowerLighter of Primus. I have fallen in love with this simple, yet wonderful tool. It will make any fire a joy to start, from lighting a simple tea light and your stove to starting a warming campfire.

POWER BANK

Especially when you go out hiking or (wild) camping, a power bank is indispensable. Buy a model which can charge your phone more than once. Although it adds some weight to your backpack, there will come a time when you are glad that you brought a solid one.

CAMPING LIGHT

There are many lights on the market, from mechanically powered flashlights to fancy USB-chargeable devices or battery-powered headlights. Choose the one that fits best to your needs – but take at least one with you.

PAPER NOTEBOOK & CAMERA

On the road trips that are described in this book you will encounter many people, see many places, set foot in many historical buildings, and walk through many inspiring natural reserves. Keeping notes of your travels and making pictures is essential if you want to store your experiences for the future. Without them, this book would not have been made.

Bempton Cliffs, England, UK
54°08'57.7"N 0°10'04.4"W

2

THREE SEASONS IN ONE DAY

Experience the wild side of **the British Isles**

UNITED KINGDOM

IRELAND

The common phrase *four seasons a day* is used by many who are living on the British Isles, referring to the ever-changing weather conditions. Where four is exaggerating it a bit in my opinion, three seasons can definitely be experienced over the course of only a few hours. But changeable weather has its bright side: frequent rain showers lead to bright-blue skies, clear sunrays, and fantastic cloud formations. As a landscape photographer, I really love this.

This road trip is designed for nature lovers, hikers, and landscape photography enthusiasts – often you find these interests in the same person. And does hiking in the beautiful Connemara region or spotting seabirds at the Bempton Cliffs not sound exciting enough to you? Go wild camping in Scotland, which will provide you with a totally different experience than when you comfortably stay at picturesque castles, inns, or B&Bs. Personally, I prefer the combination of both.

With a waterproof jacket, camera, and a feeling for British humour you are good to go. And in those few cases when the weather really makes you moody, remember to start your English, Scottish or Irish breakfast with your eggs *sunny side up*.

R335 near Cregganbaun, Ireland
53°43'04.3"N 9°47'59.5"W

THE COMPLETE ROUTE

Experience the wild side of **the British Isles**

Total length
2900 km

Countries
United Kingdom | Ireland

Time
3-4 weeks

Best season
April to June and late August to end of September. Avoid the peak of summer in the Scottish Highlands due to mass tourism and the ruthless midges, especially when you go out camping in the wild. Winters are typically grey and wet.

Destinations
1 **Bempton Cliffs**
2 **North York Moors** – 80 km
3 **Edinburgh** – 310 km
4 **Cairngorm Mountains** – 220 km
5 **Isle of Skye** – 240 km
6 **Oban via Glencoe** – 260 km
7 **Loch Lomond** – 150 km
8 **Giant's Causeway** – 320 km
9 **Slieve League** – 190 km
10 **Connemara** – 290 km
11 **Cliffs of Moher** – 180 km
12 **Dublin** – 270 km
13 **Pembrokeshire Coast** – 390 km

Balance*
Nature ●●●●●
Culture ●●●●
Culinary ●●

* (max 5 dots)

SHORTER ROUTES

Along the **Wild Atlantic Way**

Total length
650 km

Time
1-2 weeks

Destinations
8 | 9 | 10 | 11

Balance
Nature ●●●●
Culture ●●
Culinary ●

Highlights of **Scotland**

Total length
900 km

Time
2 weeks

Destinations
3 | 4 | 5 | 6 | 7

Balance
Nature ●●●●●
Culture ●●●●
Culinary ●●

With your **boots in the mud**

Total length
1900 km

Time
3 weeks

Destinations
2 | 4 | 5 | 7 | 9 | 10

Balance
Nature ●●●●●
Culture ●●
Culinary ●

5
4
6
7
8
3
9
10
IRELAND
2
11
1
12
UNITED KINGDOM
13

ENGLAND

1 Bempton Cliffs

Bempton Cliffs in East Riding of Yorkshire is a stretch of coastline known for its spectacular birdlife. Northern gannets steal the spotlight among the seabirds that make this place their home, and you even have a fair chance of seeing puffins! With their colourful beaks and cute appearance, puffins arrive in spring, raising families on the steep chalk cliffs and hunting for sand eels in the sea. The majestic northern gannets soar above the cliffs before plunging into the water with their impressive dives. Other seabirds like razorbills and guillemots also nest here, making the cliffs a very busy place. With several paths and viewing platforms, you can witness the spectacle of hundreds of thousands of birds with your eyes, ears, and nose while enjoying panoramic views of the North Sea.

Northern Gannet at the Bempton Cliffs, England, UK
54°09'08.0"N 0°10'43.2"W

80 km

ENGLAND

2 North York Moors

North York Moors National Park is a natural wonderland located in the north of England. Covering over 1400 square kilometres, the park is a paradise for hikers and nature lovers, offering a vast network of trails that wind through some of the loveliest landscapes in the country. Walk a part of the Cleveland Way or explore Roseberry Topping, a distinctive hill in the landscape. And if you are tired of hiking, you can simply relax in one of the inns and enjoy some typically British meal.

EXPLORE

The seaside town of Whitby is home to the haunting ruins of Whitby Abbey, which offers a dramatic backdrop to the town's picturesque harbour.

Robin Hood's Bay is a small fishing village that breathes old-world charm, with cobbled streets, cosy pubs, and great views over the North Sea.

Whitby Abbey, England, UK
54°29'18.4"N 0°36'22.7"W

Near Ravenscar, North York Moors,
England, UK
54°25'42.4"N 0°33'56.3"W

SCOTLAND

3 Edinburgh

EXPLORE

With its gorgeous setting and views over the North Sea, Lindisfarne Castle is a well-known hotspot for landscape photographers. Those without camera will enjoy it too – Lindisfarne Castle has a rich history, and what I particularly liked about this castle is that it is still furnished in an authentic way.

No road trip through Scotland can be complete without a visit to its charming capital. Though very touristic, Edinburgh is a city that captures the heart with its architecture, cosy streets, and vibrant cultural scene. At the heart of the city lies Edinburgh Castle, a 12th-century fortress that offers nice views over the city and beyond. Enjoy one of the pubs or cafés, or dive into one of the many souvenir shops that offer just about anything and everything that can be made of wool. And if you are done with all the fellow tourists that walk the Royal Mile, then escape to the one of the beautiful green parks such as Holyrood Park.

The Royal Mile, Edinburgh, Scotland, UK
55°56'59.2"N 3°11'24.4"W

Red squirrel near Kingussie, Scotland, UK
57°06'30.2"N 3°58'32.8"W

220 km

SCOTLAND

4 Cairngorm Mountains

Just after the cosy town of Pitlochry (which is worth a short break), the landscape changes dramatically as you are entering one of the three highland plateaux that make up the Cairngorm Mountains. Climate is rough here, which is reflected by the bare and brutal landscape. Lots of outdoor activities can be done here in winter, such as ice climbing and ski touring. In summer, Cairngorms National Park is a wonderful place for hiking, which is a more accessible way to discover the area. While you wander through one of the last remnants of the Caledonian Forest, be sure to keep an eye out for the many wildlife species that you can encounter here.

EXPLORE

Those who love to see and learn more about the larger local wildlife can visit the Highland Wildlife Park in Kingussie, a large safari park where you can stand eye to eye with many of the local inhabitants of this wild region.

Forest stream in the old Caledonian Forest.

EXPLORE

If you feel scourged by rain, then warm yourself with a whisky distillery tour through the Dahlwinnie Distillery, set in the desolate landscape of the mountain village of the same name.

240 km

SCOTLAND

5 Isle of Skye

The Isle of Skye is a true gem of the Scottish Highlands, offering visitors a wealth of natural beauty and breathtaking scenery. Without doubt it is one of the best and most popular photographic locations in the whole of Europe. A hike to the famous Old Man of Storr is a must-do, but do not forget to visit the nearby Quiraing as well, which is a dramatic landscape that has been shaped over centuries by wind and rain. The hikes to those highlights may be busy during the peak season, but are nonetheless worth the sweat, frequent rain, and sore muscles afterwards!

EXPLORE

For those seeking a refreshing swim or more relaxing hike, the Fairy Pools offer crystal clear waters surrounded by imposing mountain scenery.

Fishing settlement Luib, Isle of Skye, Scotland, UK
57°16'53.3"N 6°02'16.0"W

EXPLORE

At the edge of the Isle of Skye overlooking the sea and Outer Hebrides, the lighthouse of Neist Point is a photographer's dream. Its rugged coastline and dramatic cliffs provide a stunning backdrop for your shots, regardless of the weather.

Neist Point, Isle of Skye, Scotland, UK
57°25'49.4"N 6°46'59.5"W

Near Dunvegan Castle, Isle of Skye, Scotland, UK
57°27'18.6"N 6°35'50.3"W

The infamous Scottish midges can make life outdoor quite uncomfortable. During my last visit in late August 2022, we were eaten alive minutes after parking our car with rooftop tent near Dunvegan Castle at the end of the day. We took it to our heels and drove back to Dunvegan village, asking the lady at the petrol station if she knew at what time the midges would go to sleep at night. 'In November', she said with a grin. After buying some anti-midges spray there, we returned to the photogenic spot and endured the clouds of midges by making a fire. Next morning, we had to brush our teeth while running to escape from the midges again.

260 km

SCOTLAND

6 Oban via Glencoe

The route from the Isle of Skye to Oban with a short detour to Glencoe is one of the most scenic drives in Scotland, offering great views of some of the country's most idyllic natural landscapes. As you approach Oban (which means *The Little Bay* in Gaelic), the town's harbour and bay come into view, offering a charming setting for a stroll. The town is largely built around Oban Distillery, which has been producing its well-known single malt whisky since 1794. Visitors can take a tour of the distillery and learn about the traditional production methods, as well as enjoy a tasting of the distinct salty flavours of Oban's whiskies.

EXPLORE

Along the way from the Isle of Skye to Oban, you will encounter a wealth of photographic highlights, including Eilean Donan Castle and the rugged mountains of Glencoe, along with the many other historic castles, ruins, and characteristic mountains that dot the landscape.

Oban, Scotland, UK
56°24'56.7"N 5°28'28.5"W

EXPLORE

Enjoy a lunch in Fort William, the lively come-and-go town where outdoor enthusiasts start and end their activities out in the wild.

Very touristic but popular for a good reason is the Glenfinnan Viaduct, a railway viaduct in a picturesque setting which has become particularly famous after starring in four of the eight Harry Potter movies.

Glencoe, Scotland, UK
56°39'08.7"N 4°51'24.8"W

SCOTLAND

7 Loch Lomond

After spending time in the adventurous and sometimes rough Scottish Highlands, it is time for a relaxing stop around Loch Lomond. There is one short hike which should be part of your road trip adventure through Scotland, which is the hike from Balmaha up to the grassy Conic Hill. This varied 2½-hour hike offers a spectacular view. Overlooking the dozens of boats and white sails confirms Loch Lomond's reputation as being Scotland's premier venue for water sports and is a joy to watch on a sunny day.

EXPLORE

Those who managed to miss the many Scottish Highland distilleries so far on this road trip get another chance by visiting the Glengoyne Distillery. The lack of peat smoke gives their whisky an accessible, yet rich character. Perfect for those who want to step into the world of Scottish whisky, but also valued by experienced whisky tasters.

Scottish Highland cow, Conic Hill, Scotland, UK
56°05'33.5"N 4°32'02.9"W

View on Loch Lomond, Balmaha, Scotland, UK
56°05'37.5"N 4°32'05.1"W

NORTHERN IRELAND

8 Giant's Causeway

EXPLORE

The Dark Hedges is a picturesque lane of 18th-century beech trees close to Giant's Causeway.

Giant's Causeway is a unique rock formation that has its origin in volcanic activity that occurred over 50 million years ago. It consists of around 40,000 interlocking basalt columns that form an otherworldly landscape of geometric patterns. The hexagonal columns vary in height and shape, creating a visually striking and distinctive seascape. Giant's Causeway offers numerous opportunities to capture the geometric patterns of the columns, especially during sunrise or sunset when the light enhances the natural textures.
As a remarkable example of natural geological processes, Giant's Causeway continues to fascinate scientists and visitors alike.

Giant's Causeway,
Northern Ireland, UK
55°14'25.6"N 6°30'40.8"W

The Dark Hedges,
Northern Ireland, UK
55°08'04.7"N 6°22'52.0"W

9 Slieve League

EXPLORE

Fanad Head Lighthouse, in the far north of the Isle of Ireland, is a photographic spot on the island. It is a bit of a detour coming from the direction of Letterkenny, but worth going the extra mile for photographers.

On your exploration along the Wild Atlantic Way through Ireland, Slieve League offers excellent walking opportunities over one of the most impressive coastal cliffs in Europe. Standing at a height of over 600 metres, the sheer cliffs drop dramatically down to the Atlantic Ocean, offering wonderful views and a sense of exhilarating vertigo that make you feel if you are standing on the edge of the world. The countless sheep and white houses that dot the landscape form a cute contrast to the wild ocean on the other side.

Slieve League, Ireland
54°37'50.0"N 8°40'29.5"W

IRELAND

10 Connemara

The wild and rugged terrain of Connemara National Park is a mixture of mountains, bogs, lakes, and heathland. One of the highlights is a hike to Diamond Hill, which takes you through rocky terrain and offers ever-changing views of the Connemara landscape. From the summit, you can take in panoramic views of the Atlantic Ocean, the Twelve Bens Mountain range, and the surrounding valleys and lakes. Take a windproof and rainproof jacket with you though, as Connemara is notorious for its wind and frequent rain showers.

EXPLORE

The road trip leg to Connemara National Park gives you the opportunity to drive one of Europe's most surprisingly beautiful stretches of tarmac that should not be missed! Take the detour and drive the R335 from Cregganbaun to Aasleagh. You will not regret it.

Connemara National Park, Ireland
53°32'53.5"N 9°54'52.9"W

One of the many wild views
in the Connemara region in Ireland.

180 km

IRELAND

11 Cliffs of Moher

EXPLORE

Sky Road near Clifden is a great coastal road that is only a little detour on your way to the Cliffs of Moher, but worth to drive!

The Cliffs of Moher feature in any top-10 list of places to visit in Ireland, and rightfully so. They are the essence of the Wild Atlantic Way. If you stand on the edge of the cliffs, you cannot be left unimpressed. The steep cliffs rise from the Atlantic Ocean up to more than 200 metres tall. Formed over 300 million years ago, the various rock layers of the cliffs reveal the timeline of Ireland's geological history. No matter the weather, this is a spectacular site to visit. But if you are lucky, you can maybe snap a picture of the cliffs softly illuminated by the sun setting over the Atlantic Ocean at the end of the day.

Cliffs of Moher, Ireland
52°58'50.8"N 9°25'38.9"W

IRELAND

12 Dublin

Dublin, the lively capital of Ireland where almost one-third of the population of the country lives, is the last stop in Ireland on this road trip. A highlight in Dublin is the Old Library at Trinity College, home to the famous Book of Kells. This 9th-century manuscript is considered one of the most beautiful books in the world, which you can see in person during a visit to the library. It will be one of the most impressive libraries you will ever visit!

Trinity College Library, Dublin, Ireland
53°20'38.3"N 6°15'23.9"W

Skomer Island, Wales, UK
51°44'10.8"N 5°17'01.8"W

390 km

WALES

13 Pembrokeshire Coast

With its towering cliffs, sandy beaches, rocky coves, and photogenic harbours, Pembrokeshire Coast National Park offers the most varied coastal scenery in the whole of the UK. One of the highlights of the park is a visit to Skomer Island, a wildlife haven that is home to thousands of seabirds, including puffins, guillemots, and razorbills. If you are lucky enough, you can take a boat trip to the island to observe the birds up close. If you want to be sure to spot puffins, then go in spring – puffins are breeding between early April and the end of June, after which they head off to spend the rest of the year on the Atlantic Ocean.

Skomer Island, Wales, UK
51°44'18.6"N 5°16'58.1"W

A sunlit and moonlit evening
at Pembrokeshire Coast National Park.

Personal notes

The destinations that compose this road trip have been carefully chosen based on my journeys to the UK and Ireland in 2011, 2015, 2016, 2017, and 2022.

As a landscape photographer and nature lover, the British Isles – and Scotland in particular – have always been a fantastic destination for me. Though weather can be unforgiving, the scenery and dramatic cloud formations make up for any discomfort caused by rain or harsh winds. The unrivalled natural landscapes in this relatively accessible part of Europe make it unique. Being out in nature shooting awe-inspiring photographs of some of Europe's most impressive landscapes and enjoying a hot meal at one of the many places that serve *The Best Fish and Chips in Town* in the evening? This can only be experienced in this part of Europe.

View on Whitby, North York Moors,
England, UK
54°26'25.8"N 0°39'51.2"W

Inverfarigaig, Loch Ness, Scotland, UK
57°16'57.2"N 4°27'05.8"W

Essential tips for **camping out in the wild**

Wild camping is a wonderful adventure! This travel style is not permitted everywhere in Europe, but Scotland and Scandinavia – both of which are covered in this book – are two great destinations to wake up from your (rooftop) tent in the middle of nowhere. With these tips you are good to go and immerse yourself in nature at its very best.

CHECK OUT THE RESTRICTIONS FOR WILD CAMPING

In Scotland and Scandinavia, you can pitch your tent almost anywhere you like as long as you stick to some basic rules. Read the Scottish Outdoor Access Code for Scotland and the guidelines to the Freedom (or Right) to Roam in Sweden and Norway before you go, so you can choose the right spot responsibly.

PREPARE FOR THE WEATHER – AND THE BUGS

The only shelter you have is your tent (and your car if you travel with a rooftop tent or campervan). Even during the warmer half of the year, nights can be cold and damp. Prepare appropriately with thermal underwear, warm socks, and insect repellent.

BUILD A FIRE SAFELY

Provided you do it safely by building a stone ring at a safe distance from the forest, a campfire makes a huge difference in your wild camping experience! Building a fire from scratch takes some effort and practice, but you can help yourself by bringing along some firelighters and a good lighter (check out the gear ideas on page 48). When you are going out in the field or forest to gather branches and wood, remember that birch is the best wood to start your fire with.

FIND THE RIGHT SPOT

This is probably the most difficult part for many. Apart from using apps and suggestions from others, I challenge you to learn how to read maps and aerial images to find the best spots on your own. Switch to the aerial view in your favourite mapping application, and then look out for open spots in the forest, hidden pathways (without houses at the end) and secret places near a lake or fjord, and you will be delighted to see how much it helps in your search for a place to spend the night.

PREPARE THE RIGHT CAMPFIRE DINNER

Since I only use a simple gas stove for cooking, my dishes are simple yet tasty. Often, I go for a pasta with olive oil, sundried tomatoes, courgette, anchovies and parmesan cheese, or I choose to warm up a ready-to-use soup with some bread if rain is spoiling the fun. Be creative with simple and pure ingredients – one of the reasons I love the Italian cuisine.

Vliehors, Vlieland, the Netherlands
53°13'24.5"N 4°52'28.4"E

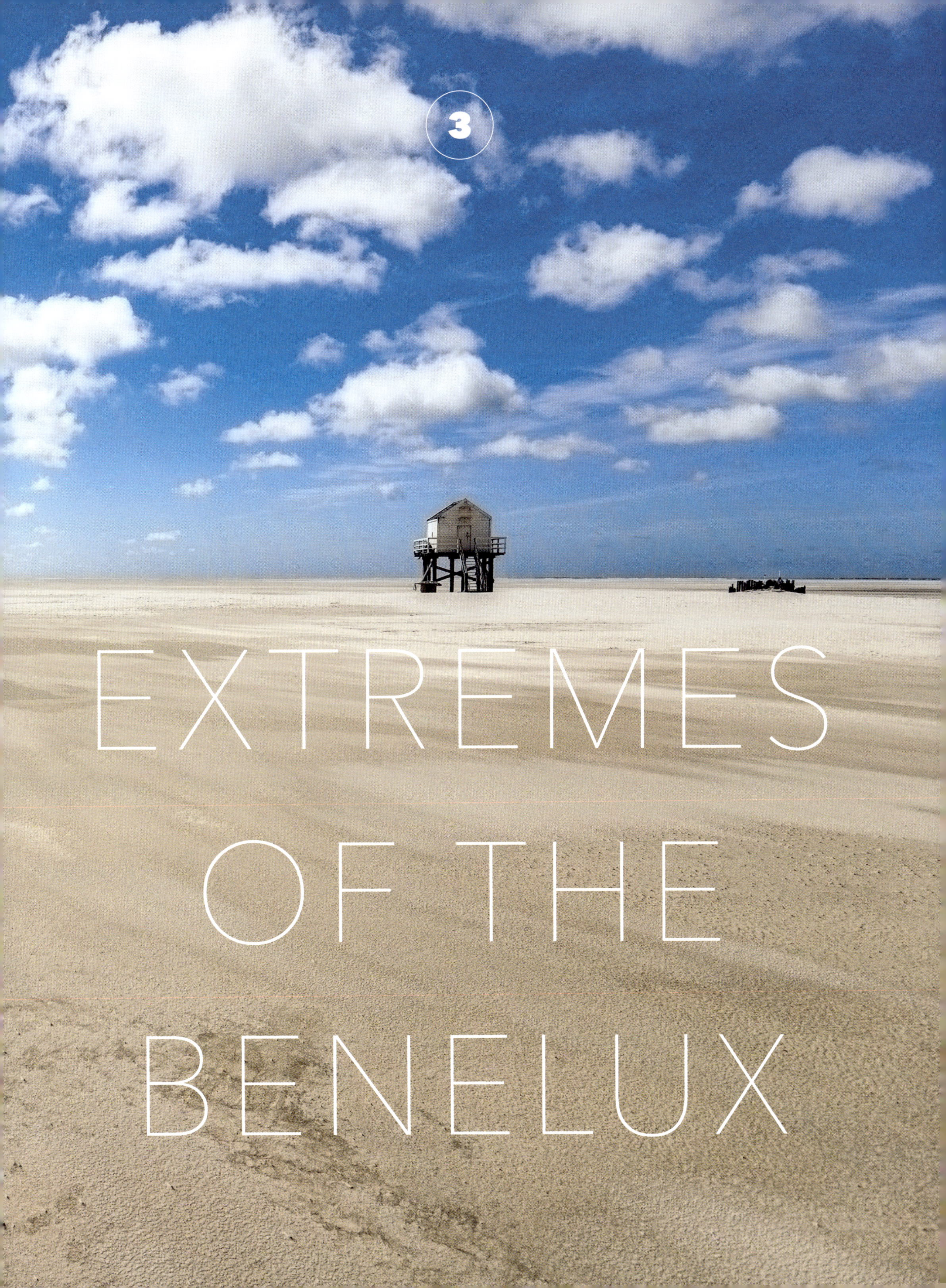

3

EXTREMES OF THE BENELUX

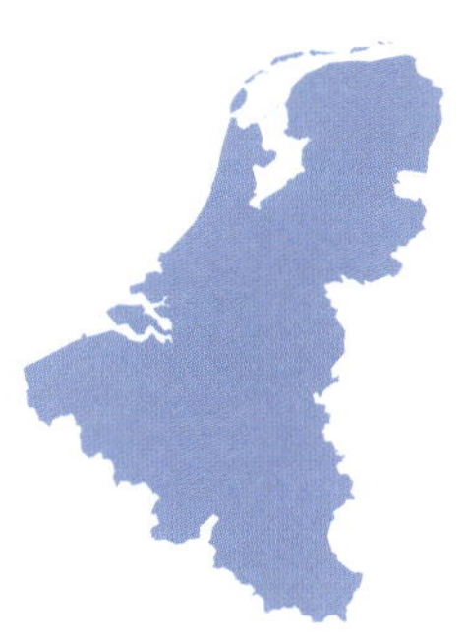

Stunning natural scenes and **metropolitan splendour**

Being Dutch and having lived most of my life in the Netherlands, what would a travel photography book be without a few words on the region I call home? The Benelux – Belgium, the Netherlands, and Luxembourg – are three small countries that show many contrasts in a small area. Walk over endless beaches on the islands of the Wadden Sea while watching seals and gulls. Go outdoor on one of the many adventurous activities in the Ardennes. Inhale the modern and worldly city life of Rotterdam with its nickname *Manhattan of Europe*. Or lose yourself on a hike in the mountainous forests of Luxembourg and enjoy a classy dinner in the namesake capital afterwards.

This short road trip is a journey of the Benelux' extremes and contrasts and takes you from enchanting nature scenes to worldly metropolitan splendour. All in just over 500 kilometres of driving. Stay in any of the four stops for as long as you like – each of these destinations is worth spending a holiday on its own.

LUXEMBOURG

BELGIUM

THE NETHERLANDS

Këppeglee, Luxembourg
49°49'49.1"N 6°19'24.2"E

THE COMPLETE ROUTE

Stunning natural scenes and **metropolitan splendour**

Total length
550 km

Countries
Luxembourg | Belgium | The Netherlands

Time
1-2 weeks

Best season
April to October is the best time, but this road trip can be made all year round.

Destinations
1 **Little Switzerland**
2 **Durbuy & Belgian Ardennes** – 130 km
3 **Rotterdam** – 250 km
4 **Texel** & **Vlieland** – 170 km

Balance*
Nature ●●●
Culture ●●●
Culinary ●●●●

* (max 5 dots)

4
THE NETHERLANDS
3
BELGIUM
2
LUXEMBOURG
1

EXPLORE

Less than an hour drive from Little Switzerland lies the Saarschleife, a schoolbook example of a meander. You can admire this bend in the river Saar from the viewing platform Cloef.

Berdorf, Luxembourg
49°49'01.5"N 6°21'17.1"E

LUXEMBOURG

1 Little Switzerland

Little Switzerland, a nickname for the region around Müllerthal, is an area of surprising natural beauty in the Benelux. The rolling hills with their rocky sculptures and winding rivers offer a perfect setting to relax while wandering in nature. For those who love hiking and climbing, the region offers an abundance of trails and routes to explore. The most famous network of hiking routes is the Müllerthal Trail, which takes you up and down through forests and imposing rock formations. Climbing enthusiasts can challenge themselves on the towering sandstone walls of Berdorf, but those that like to keep their feet on the ground will find enough rocky challenges too – many narrow passages and even some exciting underground caverns are found in the region.

EXPLORE

Luxembourg City is close to the Müllerthal region and worth a visit. Walk up Le Chemin de la Corniche for a good overview of Luxembourg's capital.

Berdorf, Luxembourg
49°49'55.6"N 6°20'40.8"E

Hohllay Cave, Berdorf, Luxembourg
49°48'54.9"N 6°21'31.7"E

Château de Durbuy, Belgium
50°21'11.4"N 5°27'19.7"E

BELGIUM

2 Durbuy & Belgian Ardennes

Set in the heart of the Belgian Ardennes, Durbuy is a tiny medieval city with winding cobblestone streets and historic buildings. The town is known for its gourmet cuisine, little boutiques, lively markets, and as being a hub for outdoor adventures. From kayaking to cycling and hiking, on and along the Ourthe River you can do it all. Apart from going back and forth along the river, you can also go up or down in the area. Visit the caves of Hotton for an underground adventure or climb up the nearby limestone walls if you are a rock climber.

EXPLORE

On your way to the Belgian Ardennes, make a stop in the small town of Esch-sur-Sûre and enjoy the fantastic view on the nearby Lac de la Haute-Sûre from the viewing spot Runtschelt.

Hotton, Belgium
50°15'58.5"N 5°27'30.0"E

THE NETHERLANDS

3 Rotterdam

EXPLORE

The nearby cities Schiedam and Delft feature old-Dutch architecture including the famous canals, and they are a joy to stroll through.

Although world-class port city Rotterdam has plenty of museums, galleries, and other cultural places to visit, nothing beats its stunning skyline. Approach the city from the Van Brienenoordbrug that leads the motorway A20 over the Nieuwe Maas (New Meuse). Then take the Maasboulevard to the heart of the city, which is a spectacular avenue to drive, especially one hour after sunset. Next to the modern highlights of Rotterdam, a walk through the old Delfshaven district with its authentic houses or a stroll around the Entrepot-haven will be enjoyed by everyone. And if you have lost the overview: visit the touristic yet impressive viewing platform of the Euromast, which offers fabulous views on one of Europe's most exciting cities.

Kop van Zuid, Rotterdam,
the Netherlands
51°54'08.3"N 4°29'13.1"E

EXPLORE

Those who enjoy a cosmopolitan experience should visit the peninsula Kop van Zuid, which features various luxurious residential towers and Cruise Port Rotterdam – gigantic cruise ships dock here multiple times a week. Do not forget to also cross the Rijnhavenbrug (also known as the *Hoerenloper*, a connection to its red-light district past) to explore Katendrecht, a sparkling hotspot where the past meets the future.

Near Entrepothaven, Rotterdam,
the Netherlands
51°54'24.3"N 4°30'19.5"E

For more than two years I have lived in the heart of Rotterdam, and I have worked in this city for a significant part of my career. This means that I look at this city not only through the eyes of a traveller, but also as a resident. Rotterdam is a city that you will appreciate more and more as time goes by. The mentality, the contrasts in architecture, the genuine atmosphere that is both rough and honest, and the spectacular, world-class skyline – just for its photographic potential alone, Rotterdam deserves a place in this book.

Rotterdam-Zuid,
the Netherlands
51°54'18.2"N 4°29'17.0"E

170 km

THE NETHERLANDS

4 Texel & Vlieland

A combined trip to Texel and Vlieland is a great way to experience the best of the Dutch Wadden Sea. Texel is the largest of the Dutch Wadden Sea islands and is known for its long sandy beaches, little villages, and mixed nature. You can hike or cycle through the nature reserves, such as De Slufter or De Schorren. On the island you can spot rare bird species or enjoy the lush fields of wild hyacinths in the coastal forests. Vlieland, on the other hand, is the smallest of the inhabited Dutch Wadden Sea islands and is known for its tranquil atmosphere and unspoiled nature. You can explore the island by bike or on foot, as cars are not allowed on the island. Of particular interest is the Vliehors, a vast expanse of sand dunes that resembles an endless desert – 20 million square metres of opportunities to spot seals, explore military structures and to find the *Drenkelingenhuisje* in the far distance.

EXPLORE

Whether you are a beer enthusiast or not, a visit to Texel's brewery guarantees a cosy afternoon in the world of beer making.

Eierland Lighthouse, Texel, the Netherlands
53°10'55.1"N 4°51'08.9"E

‘Vlieland is the smallest of the inhabited Dutch Wadden Sea islands and is known for its tranquil atmosphere and unspoiled nature’

Oost-Vlieland, the Netherlands
53°17’45.5”N 5°04’26.6”E

EXPLORE

In summer you can take the small passenger boat from Texel to Vlieland. Alternatively, you can also go back to Den Helder and drive over the well-known Afsluitdijk to Harlingen, and take the ferry to Vlieland from there.

Personal notes

You cannot possibly cover the variety in landscapes and cultural heritage of the Benelux in one or two weeks. And even if you think you have seen its diversity after decades of living here, the Benelux still holds many surprises.

Recently, I exchanged the busy Randstad for Wageningen, at the edge of the Veluwe. I did not know the region before moving there in March 2023, but I have been very surprised to find such a hidden gem in the Netherlands. From the Wageningse Berg overlooking Batavia and the river Nederrijn to the soft heathlands in the forests of Bennekom and the green blankets covering Renkums Beekdal, all these fantastic scenes are now within walking distance from my new home. It proves once again that you do not have to travel far to feel like a traveller.

Bennekomse Bos, Veluwe, the Netherlands
51°59'49.1"N 5°41'45.7"E

Skyline of Rotterdam, the Netherlands
Exposure time: 30 sec | Aperture: f/8 | ISO 100
51°54'18.5"N 4°29'03.7"E

Capturing **the perfect blue**

My favourite photographic time of the day is the blue hour, which is a brief period of twilight before sunrise or after sunset when the sky takes on a rich blue hue. During this time, the light is soft and diffuse, creating a peaceful and serene atmosphere. The blue hour is also a great time to take long exposure shots of cityscapes, landscapes, and architecture, as the contrast between the deep blue sky and warm artificial lights can create powerful visual effects. Here are my basic tips to start photographing during the dark part of the day yourself.

BRING A TRIPOD ALONG

Photographing properly during the blue hour and at night is impossible without a tripod, so if you want to take good shots of skylines and the starry night, be sure to bring some sturdy object with you that can be attached to your camera.

GO THE MANUAL ROAD

If you want to take eye-catching shots after sunset, you need to understand how to set your camera manually. Depending on what you want to achieve, put it in aperture priority mode, shutter priority mode, or fully manual.

GO FOR LONG EXPOSURES

Long exposures tend to perfectly blend water, clouds, and any other movement. This gives a special effect to your pictures. Take an exposure of at least 15 seconds to achieve this effect, but keep experimenting in your situation, as you might need a shorter or longer exposure in some cases.

KEEP CONTROL OF YOUR ISO

High ISO values produce more noise in your images, so during the blue hour you can best keep this value as low as possible. Another advantage of a low ISO is that the required shutter speed goes up, which makes it easier to get the long exposure effect in your images. But low ISO values are not always the best option. The faint light of stars is not bright enough to be captured with a low ISO. Therefore, if you are shooting a starry night sky, tune up your ISO value up to ISO 800 or more to see the stars in your images.

PLAY WITH LENS APERTURE

Depending on your lens, you can create starburst effects in light poles and other sources of light. Use an aperture of f/8 to f/16 to achieve this effect. I do not recommend smaller apertures like f/22 because they significantly reduce the optical quality of your photos (lenses typically have a sweet spot between f/8 and f/11).

POST PROCESS!

Editing your images is indispensable if you want to capture the perfect blue on your photo. Especially when you shoot in RAW, images have not been processed yet to reveal the colours of the scene that you saw with your own eyes. Play around with the sliders that control brightness, contrast, shadows, highlights, colours, and details, and you will be impressed by the results. Or blend multiple exposures together to create HDR (High Dynamic Range) images that reveal the deepest shadows and brightest highlights of a scene for even more striking effects. Do not forget to straighten the horizon and frame the image properly, though – a good composition is equally important.

On the A-397 between Marbella
and Ronda, Spain
36°35'10.9"N 5°04'06.0"W

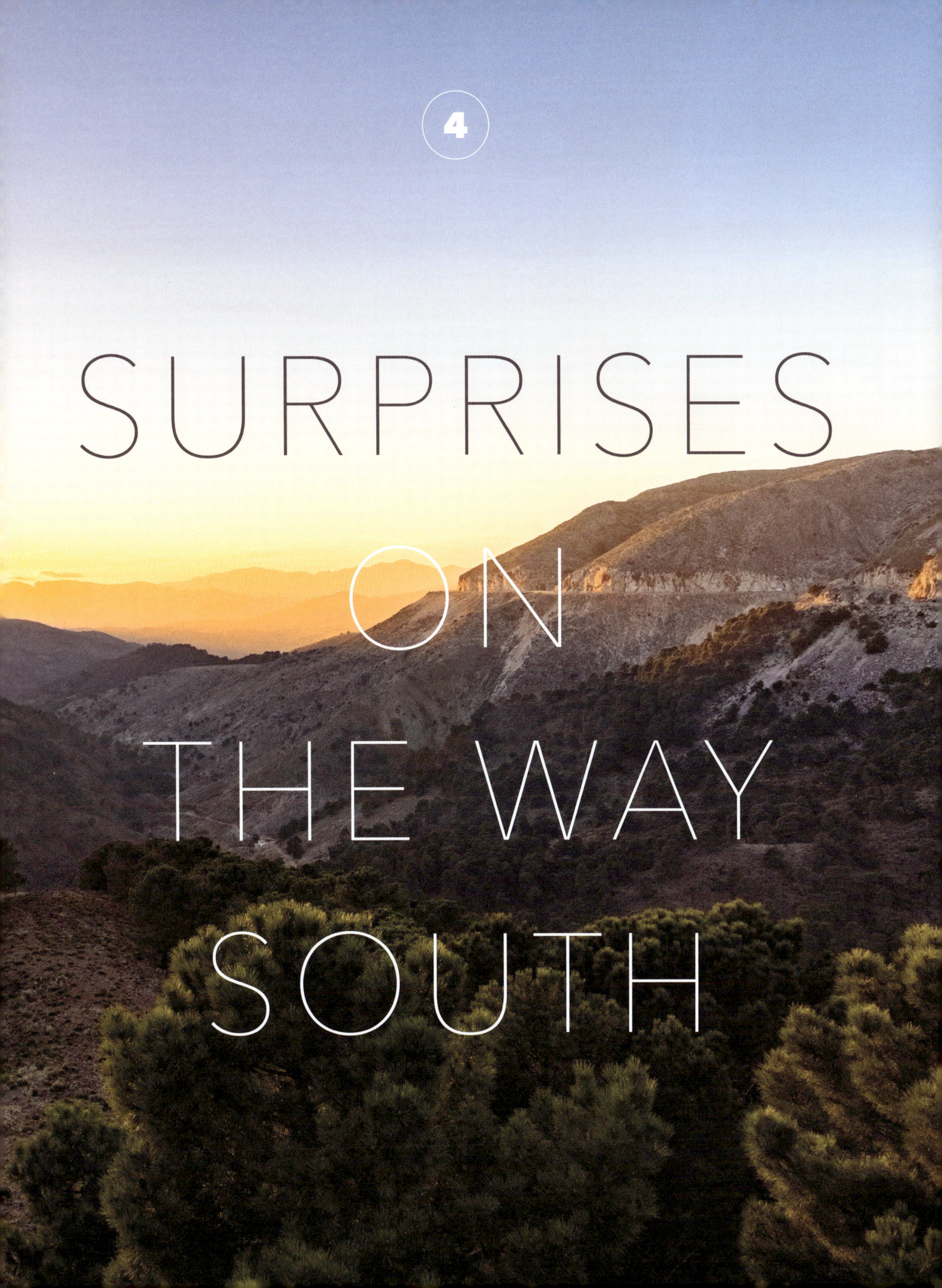

4 SURPRISES ON THE WAY SOUTH

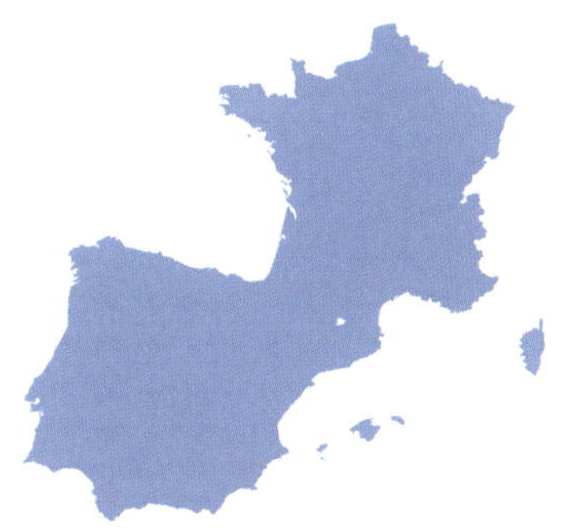

From inland surprises to **brilliant shores**

Even seasoned travellers to France and the Iberian Peninsula can still be surprised by the beauty of some of the lesser-known regions in the southwestern part of Europe. Starting high up in the Massif Central in the heart of France, this road trip will treat you with medieval and modern architecture, culinary heritage, and some special nature reserves that are not yet discovered by the masses.

Two memories of my first road trip through Southwest Europe will always stay with me: the woody smell of wine corks in La Rioja with snow-capped mountains shaping the horizon, and the spectacle of a group of pigs running between the cork oaks next to a seemingly endless road in the middle of nowhere in Extremadura. Both destinations are part of this road trip and emphasise the surprises that are found far away from the famous Costas of Southwest Europe.

This road trip is for those travellers who like the comfort of the sun, enjoy food and local culture, but at the same time are open to unexpected experiences and surprisingly beautiful scenery. The more you go inland, the more interesting it will become.

FRANCE

SPAIN

PORTUGAL

Roman aqueduct of Segovia, Spain
40°56'54.2"N 4°07'05.9"W

THE COMPLETE ROUTE

From inland surprises to **brilliant shores**

Total length
2800 km

Countries
France | Spain | Portugal

Time
3-4 weeks

Best season
September to May. Summers tend to be (increasingly) hot. Some of the mountainous destinations may not be fully accessible in winter.

Destinations
1 **Monts du Cantal**
2 **Cahors** – 170 km
3 **Ordesa Valley** – 380 km
4 **La Rioja** – 280 km
5 **Madrid** – 320 km
6 **Monfragüe** – 250 km
7 **Sintra-Cascais Natural Park** – 400 km
8 **Southwest Alentejo** & **Vicentine Coast** – 320 km
9 **Ardales** & **El Caminito del Rey** – 470 km
10 **Sierra Nevada** – 210 km

Balance*
Nature ● ● ● ●
Culture ● ● ● ●
Culinary ● ● ● ● ●

* (max 5 dots)

SHORTER ROUTES

The best of **inland Spain**

Total length
1550 km

Time
2 weeks

Destinations
3 | 4 | 5 | 6 | 9 | 10

Balance
Nature ● ● ● ●
Culture ● ● ● ●
Culinary ● ● ● ●

A circle around the **Iberian Peninsula**

Total length
1650 km

Time
2-3 weeks

Destinations
5 | 6 | 7 | 8 | 9 | 10

Balance
Nature ● ● ● ●
Culture ● ● ●
Culinary ● ● ● ●

Wine & Dine in the **South**

Total length
1850 km

Time
2-3 weeks

Destinations
2 | 4 | 5 | 7 | 8

Balance
Nature ● ●
Culture ● ● ● ●
Culinary ● ● ● ● ●

FRANCE
PORTUGAL
SPAIN
1
2
3
4
5
6
7
8
9
10

Monts du Cantal, Massif Central,
France
45°06'31.9"N 2°40'40.2"E

FRANCE

1 Monts du Cantal

The open landscape of the Monts du Cantal – which is part of a much larger highland known as Massif Central – has been shaped by an enormous stratovolcano formed here roughly 13 million years ago. After its last eruption 2 million years ago, erosion by wind and water slowly transformed the rough lava-scarred landscape to the rolling hills and wildflower valleys that we see today. Embarking on a hike to the panoramic viewpoint on the Puy Mary is a perfect way to experience the landscape. Monts du Cantal's wide views and mild climate make it an excellent destination for both hikers and cyclists, especially those who like to conclude the day with a classical French dinner and some tasty Cantal cheese for dessert.

Le Puy Mary, Monts du Cantal, France
45°06'39.0"N 2°40'27.6"E

Pont Valentré, Cahors, France
44°26'40.7"N 1°25'57.7"E

170 km

FRANCE

2 Cahors

Those who stroll through the narrow cobblestone streets of Cahors will soon discover that this medieval town has a strong connection to the Malbec grapes that thrive in the region's clay and limestone soils. Cahors' story of wine is one of resilience and tradition. Despite challenges and setbacks such as the damage during the Great French Wine Blight, the winemakers of this region have persevered. The dark, robust red wines of Cahors are characterised by their deep colour and bold flavours, for which they have earned a distinguished place among wine enthusiasts. But Cahors has more to offer than wine. Its medieval streets, ancient architecture, and charming riverside setting are perfect for a relaxing stop. Walk over the Valentré Bridge, an architectural masterpiece that spans the Lot River, or take a closer look at Cahors Cathedral. Or simply settle down in one of the cosy cafés to enjoy a coffee with some *pâtisseries*.

One of the many vineyards near Cahors, France.

The trail through Ordesa Valley, Spain
42°38'39.6"N 0°00'32.2"E

380 km

SPAIN

3 Ordesa Valley

The scenic Ordesa Valley, which is part of the larger Ordesa and Monte Perdido National Park, gained its distinctive shape during and after the last Ice Age. As the immense ice masses of glaciers advanced and retreated, they carved deep U-shaped valleys, of which Ordesa Valley is a schoolbook example. The Ordesa River, flowing through the heart of the valley, also played a crucial role in shaping its landscape. Over time, the river carved its path, etching through the layers of sedimentary rocks, and creating the imposing gorge that characterises the Ordesa Valley today. The hike through the valley leads through spectacular terrain and is considered one of the highlights of the Pyrenees.

280 km

SPAIN

4 La Rioja

EXPLORE

Visit the Vivanco Museum of Wine Culture in Briones, even if you do not like wine. It showcases the region's winemaking traditions through exhibits on grape cultivation, winemaking tools, and historical artifacts. It is an interesting journey through the centuries-long relationship between La Rioja and its wines.

Welcome to La Rioja, where wine flows like a river and grapevines stretch as far as the eye can see. The region's winemaking heritage dates back centuries, and its vineyards deliver distinctive red wines. You can explore the numerous wineries, indulge in wine tastings, and immerse yourself in the rich history and techniques of winemaking. But while grapes typically need sun and a bit of warmth, La Rioja also has a surprising winter secret up its sleeve. Valdezcaray is the region's ski resort, which offers routes at various levels in a panoramic mountain setting. La Rioja simply is lovely in every season and in every weather. What Tuscany is to Italy, La Rioja is to Spain. Beware that the Spanish start their dinner much later, though.

Vineyard garden of Vivanco Museum, Briones, Spain
42°32'24.8"N 2°46'42.5"W

EXPLORE

If you have plenty of time for a longer stop, a visit to Bilbao is highly recommended, which has a unique combination of modern and historical architecture. The Guggenheim Museum is one of its highlights.

Pay a visit to Segovia, which lies between La Rioja and Madrid. This small city is famous for its Roman aqueduct, which runs straight through the city centre as a dominant wall.

Zarratón, Spain
42°30'59.5"N 2°52'47.7"W

320 km

SPAIN

5 Madrid

EXPLORE

Near Madrid lies the Royal Site of San Lorenzo de El Escorial, which is one of the most impressive buildings in Europe. It is an architectural masterpiece that captures the grandeur and historical significance of Spain.

Well known as the capital of Spain, but far less touristic than its coastal counterpart Barcelona, Madrid is a great city stop for your road trip. When I visited Madrid in December 2017, I was surprised by the relaxed atmosphere for a capital this size. City lovers can stay here for a couple of days, but if you are only here for a short time, I recommend visiting the Glass Palace of El Retiro, which is an inspiring building made of glass set in an iron framework. It is located in the Buen Retiro Park, a tranquil green space in the heart of Madrid.

San Lorenzo de El Escorial, Spain
40°35'15.0"N 4°09'00.2"W

Palacio de Cristal, Madrid, Spain
40°24'49.1"N 3°40'55.2"W

View from Castillo de Monfragüe,
Extremadura, Spain
39°49'41.6"N 6°03'07.7"W

250 km

SPAIN

6 Monfragüe

The Extremadura region in the western part of Spain offers a surprising *middle-of-nowhere* experience – especially road EX-208 through Monfragüe National Park and further southwards. Spacious fields of cork oak trees with wild Black Iberian pigs running around freely, with nothing but a desolate road that stretches endlessly in front of you. This is the unexplored Spain! The special nature reserve Monfragüe itself is more touristic, but for a good reason. The landscape created over time by the Tagus River is not only a scenic spot, but it also home to various birds of prey. Keep your eyes peeled for the majestic vultures, who are soaring endlessly above the cliffs with their wide wingspans and dark plumage.

Cork oaks along the EX-208,
Extremadura, Spain
39°45'20.4"N 6°00'14.4"W

'Spacious fields of cork oak trees with wild Black Iberian pigs running around freely, with nothing but a desolate road that stretches endlessly in front of you. This is the unexplored Spain!'

Griffon vulture, Salto del Gitano, Monfragüe, Spain
39°49'44.2"N 6°03'27.6"W

PORTUGAL

7 Sintra-Cascais Natural Park

EXPLORE

If you have the time, plan an additional stop at Lisbon, the capital of Portugal. Whatever the season or weather, you will be surprised by its hospitality and cheerful atmosphere.

Sintra-Cascais Natural Park is a romantic destination near Lisbon, Portugal's capital. The park is nestled between the town of Sintra, known for its fairytale-like palaces, and the coastal town of Cascais. The diverse landscape is a mixture of rich forests, rolling hills, and dramatic cliffs. The region is dotted with remarkable palaces, including the colourful Pena Palace with its turrets and towers, and the mysterious Quinta da Regaleira with its underground structures and beautiful gardens. And if you are not afraid of heights, capture the panoramic views from the cliffs of Cabo da Roca, Europe's westernmost point.

Sintra-Cascais Natural Park, Portugal
38°46'40.4"N 9°29'51.8"W

Quinta da Regaleira, Portugal
38°47'46.8"N 9°23'45.6"W

Castelejo Beach, Portugal
37°06'06.9"N 8°56'43.1"W

320 km

PORTUGAL

8 Southwest Alentejo & Vicentine Coast

Portugal's southwestern coast is an almost endless route of peaceful beaches, excellent surfing spots, good seafood, and plenty of scenic spots. Whether you decide to stop at Vila do Bispo at the southern end of the Portuguese coastline or in any of the other places along the coast, you will find great locations to relax and enjoy the coastal atmosphere. Be sure to visit Castelejo Beach, which is a perfect place to enjoy the ocean view just before and after sunset – the golden and blue hour, respectively.

Surfers in the Atlantic Ocean,
Torre de Aspa, Portugal
37°05'48.5"N 8°57'05.6"W

470 km

SPAIN

9 Ardales & El Caminito del Rey

Near the little town of Ardales in the heart of Andalusia lies El Caminito del Rey – The King's Little Path – one of the most spectacular walking trails in Europe. It is a scenic walkway that winds its way along the sheer walls of the El Chorro Gorge, offering breathtaking views and an unforgettable adventure. Originally constructed in the early 20th century as a service route for hydroelectric power workers, El Caminito del Rey gained a reputation for its perilous state and was closed for many years. However, after a comprehensive renovation, it was reopened in 2015, showcasing its former glory while ensuring safety measures for visitors.

Ardales, Spain
36°52'42.3"N 4°50'51.9"W

EXPLORE

Roughly 50 kilometres before you reach the town of Ardales, you will arrive in Ronda, known for the Puente Nuevo Bridge spanning the El Tajo Gorge. Although touristic, this is definitely worth a stop along the way.

Near Ardales lies the nature reserve El Torcal. Its unique limestone formations, shaped by millions of years of erosion, create a surreal landscape that seems straight out of a fantasy world.

El Caminito del Rey, Spain
36°54'58.4"N 4°46'25.2"W

Two years after the reopening of El Caminito del Rey, when I visited it, I did not know that it was renovated recently. I did not do my homework well enough, apparently. So we prepared for the rough version of El Caminito del Rey with a via ferrata set, helmet and all the courage we could muster up. But the via ferrata set remained untouched and much courage was not required – in its renovated state El Caminito del Rey is accessible to almost anyone, provided you are not afraid of heights. We were both laughing and a bit disappointed at the same time, but looking back I am very happy we did not embark on that old via ferrata – it would have been far too extreme and dangerous.

El Caminito del Rey, Spain
36°55'50.4"N 4°47'07.9"W

SPAIN

10 Sierra Nevada

The Sierra Nevada, a giant mountain range in the south of Spain, is home to one of the most prominent peaks of Europe, the Mulhacén. Although high alpine in terms of elevation, the hike itself to the summit of this majestic mountain does not require special alpine skills. Experienced mountain hikers can reach the roof of Europe in one day from the village of Capileira, albeit a long and straining hike. But on your way to the summit of 3482 metres, the views are simply unforgettable! Whether you want to reach the summit of the Mulhacén or admire its silhouette from a distance, the Sierra Nevada is a tranquil escape in nature all year round.

En route to the Mulhacén, Sierra Nevada, Spain
37°03'09.0"N 3°19'05.5"W

Sierra Nevada National Park, Spain
37°01’53.7”N 3°18’47.6”W

SOLI
DEO
GLORI

Personal notes

This chapter has been the most difficult for me to compose. There are so many great routes through France, Spain, Andorra, and Portugal all the way to Gibraltar on the southern edge of Europe. There are so many wonderful National Parks, cities, coastal landscapes, mountain ranges, deserted inland roads, and picturesque villages. From the peculiar rock formations of Praia de Augas Santas in Galicia to the colourful slopes of Porto and the spotless white mills of La Mancha that make a perfect contrast with a bright-blue sky, the Iberian Peninsula has it all – but unfortunately you cannot do it all in one trip. The destinations that I have selected in this road trip (based on trips in 2012, 2017, 2018, and 2019) make for a varied adventure, with totally different natural landscapes, cities in various sizes, and some of Europe's most surprising destinations that have made a lasting impression on me. Feel free to turn left or right wherever you see fit, there is no wrong turn anywhere.

Summit of the Mulhacén (3482 m),
Sierra Nevada, Spain
37°03'12.7"N 3°18'39.6"W

Seven stunning day hikes
worth every step

Partially thanks to my dog Alex, I love to walk and on average I cover about 10 kilometres a day. Driving and walking are my two primary ways of transportation! Luckily, Europe has a large network of both gorgeous roads *and* scenic hiking trails. In the list below you find some of my favourite day hikes that are covered in the road trips in this book. The only thing you need is your best pair of walking shoes, plenty of water and food, the right clothing to beat the weather, and you are good to go on these epic hikes.

EL CAMINITO DEL REY | SPAIN

Equipped with safety gear that you will receive at the entrance, the hike through El Caminito del Rey is a class on its own. This exhilarating hike of roughly 8 kilometres through the Gaitanes Gorge in southern Spain offers magnificent views of the gorge's vertical cliffs and the rushing river below.

MOLDEN | NORWAY

Towering above the Sognefjord in Norway, the hike to the Molden is a rewarding adventure. The trail is approximately 10 kilometres long and takes around 4-6 hours to complete. It offers one of Norway's best panoramic views of the fjords and surrounding mountains.

THE OLD MAN OF STORR | UK

A popular yet splendid hike in Scotland to the famous rock formation bearing the same name. The hike up is about 4 kilometres, with roughly 300 metres elevation gain. Few short hikes offer more spectacular views than this one.

BUCURA LAKE | ROMANIA

This hike from Râușor in Romania takes you up to the alpine glacial Bucura Lake near the summit Vârful Retezat at an elevation of over 2000 metres. The scenes on this hike are untouched and show the rich biodiversity of Retezat National Park. Humanity seems far away here.

MULHACÉN | SPAIN

The longest and most straining hike in my list of favourites, the hike to the summit of Mulhacén (3482 metres) from Hoya del Portillo is one of perseverance and reward. With a distance of about 16 kilometres and an elevation gain of over 1000 metres, this tour to the roof of Europe is for experienced hikers only.

VÂRFUL TOACA | ROMANIA

From the village of Durău, the hike to Vârful Toaca is one of many outstanding views and leads past interesting rock formations, such as Căciula Dorobanțului, and the waterfall Cascada Duruitoarea on the way back. From the pine woods to the wide views, this hike is brilliant from start to end.

KRIVÁŇ | SLOVAKIA

Starting from the lake village of Štrbské Pleso, the hike to the summit of Slovakia's most gorgeous mountain first runs through forests until you reach the slopes of Kriváň. After a technically simple but straining hike you will reach the last stage, where you will find yourself using all four limbs before reaching the majestic roof of Slovakia.

The Old Man of Storr, Isle of Skye, Scotland, UK
57°30'32.8"N 6°11'02.0"W

Torneträsk, Abisko, Sweden
68°21'16.2"N 18°50'33.7"E

5
LONG DAYS & SUNNY NIGHTS

Turist Stationen
Kungsleden
Nordkalottleden
15 10 5
Skidspår
Naturstigar
Linbana
Båthamn

The winding journey to **Europe's rough North**

DENMARK

SWEDEN

NORWAY

Light forms a crucial part of Scandinavian landscapes. In summer you can enjoy one single sunny day of more than 1800 hours, which is more than a full-time working year in comparison! The famous Midnight Sun is an enchanting experience on your way to the most northernly part of mainland Europe. Imagine the sun illuminating your face from the North at two o'clock in the morning while all you can see is the sea stretching out to the North Pole and even beyond. Not just sunny shorts to be worn here, though. The elements of nature are rough and wild in Scandinavia, which – combined with the beautiful lighting conditions – is one of the reasons I fell in love with this part of Europe during my first month-long road trip back in 2010. But even in cloudy or rainy weather, Scandinavia's landscapes and wildlife stand out and few superlatives do justice to the natural scenery. From Lofoten to Stora Sjöfallet and Sognefjord, the raw beauty of Scandinavia is simply unrivalled. And as the cherry on the cake, you will have a large chance of seeing reindeer, a fair chance of seeing moose, and if you are as lucky as I have been, even a brown bear next to the road.

Scandinavia is a destination for seekers of silence. For nature lovers, photographers and outdoor fanatics. It is one of the few places where you can camp almost everywhere you like, as long as you follow a few simple rules. This Freedom to Roam, or *allemannsretten* in Scandinavian languages, is the best invitation you can get to start camping out in the wild. Are you ready to meet the elements of nature?

Kungsleden, Abisko, Sweden
68°21'28.3"N 18°46'40.3"E

THE COMPLETE ROUTE

The winding journey to **Europe's rough North**

Total length
5000 km

Countries
Denmark | Sweden | Norway

Time
5-6 weeks

Best season
May to September. Summers are short and beware of mosquitoes and midges during the peak of summer. From the end of May to June is the best time to experience the Midnight Sun. September, on the other hand, is the most photogenic month to be out in the wild.

Destinations
1 **Mols Bjerge**
2 **Malmö** – 260 km
3 **Hallands Län** & **Gothenburg** – 270 km
4 **Mora** – 470 km
5 **Fullufjället** – 140 km
6 **Sognefjord** & **Molden** – 450 km
7 **Trollstigen** via **Ålesund** – 400 km
8 **Kristiansund** via **The Atlantic Ocean Road** – 150 km
9 **Östersund** – 460 km
10 **Skuleskogen** – 270 km
11 **Luleå** & **Gammelstad** – 430 km
12 **Jokkmokk** & **Laponia** – 250 km
13 **Abisko** – 260 km
14 **Lofoten** – 290 km
15 **Lyngen** – 390 km
16 **Alta** – 270 km
17 **The North Cape** – 240 km

Balance*
Nature ●●●●●
Culture ●●●●
Culinary ●●

* (max 5 dots)

SHORTER ROUTES

Exploring **Lapland**

Total length
1700 km

Time
2-3 weeks

Destinations
11 | 12 | 13 | 14 | 15 | 16 | 17

Balance
Nature ●●●●●
Culture ●●●●
Culinary ●

The landscape change along the **E45**

Total length
1800 km

Time
2-3 weeks

Destinations
3 | 4 | 5 | 9 | 12 | 13

Balance
Nature ●●●●
Culture ●●●
Culinary ●●

Highlights of **Southern Sweden** & **Norway**

Total length
1850 km

Time
3 weeks

Destinations
2 | 3 | 4 | 5 | 6 | 7 | 8

Balance
Nature ●●●●●
Culture ●●●●
Culinary ●●

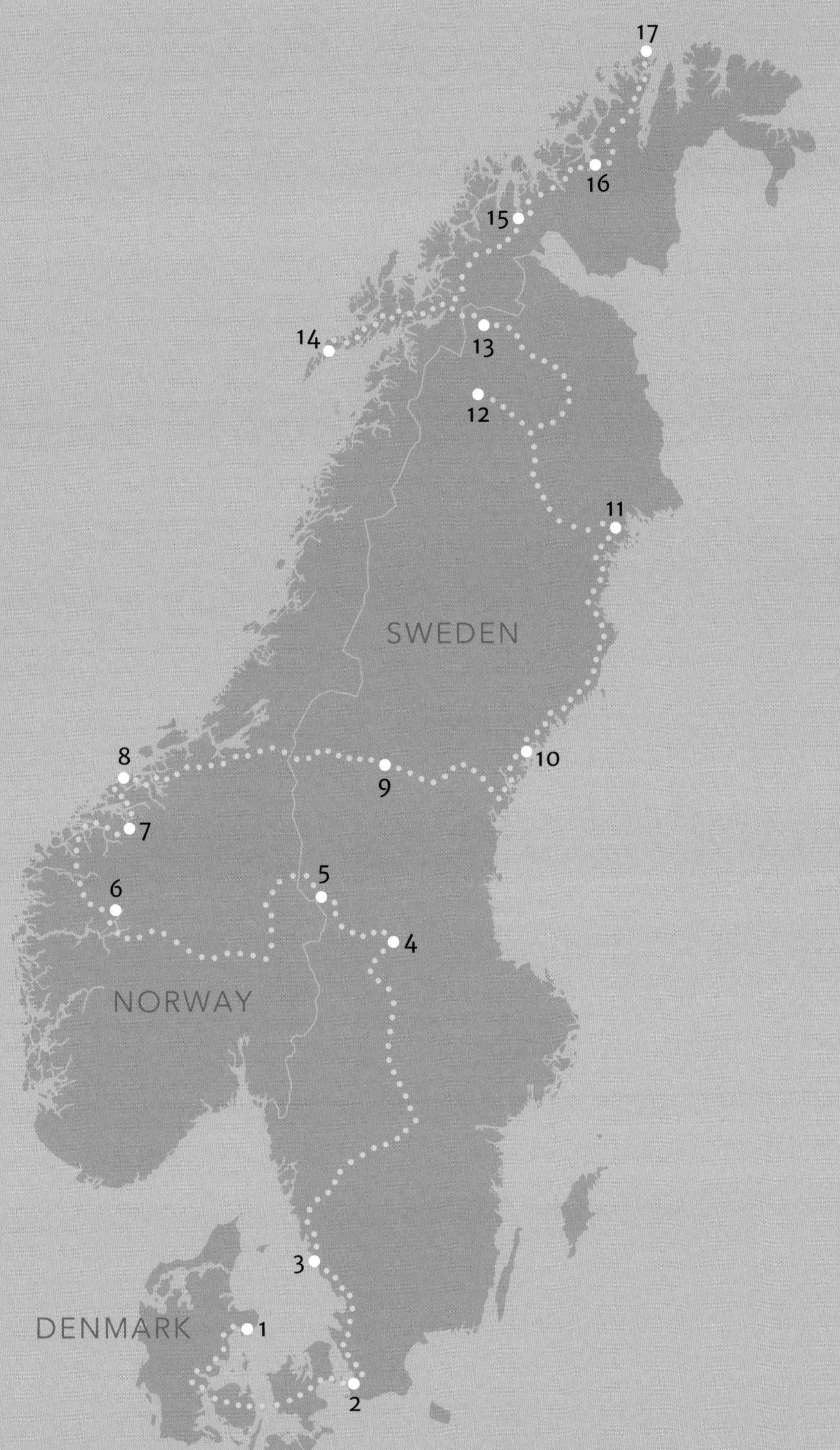
17
16
15
14
13
12
11
SWEDEN
8
9
10
7
5
6
4
NORWAY
3
DENMARK
1
2

DENMARK

1 Mols Bjerge

Mols Bjerge, a national park located in the eastern part of Jutland, is the scenic start of your road trip adventure through Scandinavia. The rolling green meadows and distant coastal views are one of my favourite landscapes in Denmark, and a small taste of what to expect on your journey through Europe's wild North. The best way to explore this region is to start a hike from the parking spot near Trehøje late in the afternoon, when the warm sun transforms the green fields into a golden blanket – a scenery that is simply too beautiful to miss.

Trehøje, Mols Bjerge, Denmark
56°12'15.4"N 10°31'47.9"E

260 km

SWEDEN

2 Malmö

The journey to Malmö crosses three significant structures: first the Little Belt Bridge, then the majestic Great Belt Bridge, and finally the imposing Øresund Bridge, which spans the strait between Denmark and Sweden (and basically connects Copenhagen to Malmö). As you cross the last bridge, you will not know where to look – the bridge structure itself and the panoramic views of the Øresund Strait equally compete for your attention. On the other side you arrive in Malmö, one of my favourite cities of Sweden. The city breathes a cosmopolitan atmosphere with its unique blend of old-world charm, innovative architecture, modern design, and maritime industry. No need to plan or prepare anything here. Simply stroll through the city, the experiences will come to you as you go.

Malmö, Sweden
55°36'28.6"N 12°59'57.2"E

Pebbles near Vassbäck, Sweden
57°19'47.1"N 12°08'17.2"E

270 km

SWEDEN

3 Hallands Län & Gothenburg

The road from Malmö to the north leads through Hallands Län, a province of Sweden that covers a large part of Sweden's western coastline. Numerous rocky beaches with countless round pebbles in various sizes form the boundary with the land and the Kattegat. Once in Gothenburg – a seaport with Dutch-style canals and an unusually square city design – grab a cup of coffee, indulge in traditional Swedish pastries like cinnamon buns, and enjoy city life while it lasts. Believe me, you will think back of this urban moment of coffee and cake when you are in the Arctic part of Scandinavia.

EXPLORE

Grimeton Radio Station in Varberg offers a unique glimpse into the history of telecommunications. This historic landmark is known for its radio masts and played a significant role in long-wave radio communication during the early 20th century.

470 km

SWEDEN

4 Mora

EXPLORE

Make a stop at Tiveden National Park on your way to Mora. This is one of most lovely forests in Scandinavia with a fairytale-like atmosphere.

North of Gothenburg the landscape clearly becomes emptier. After roughly six hours of driving, you will reach the village of Mora in the heart of Dalarna. Set in the middle of hilly woods and idyllic lakes, Mora is a perfect place to spend a few days to discover the Dalarna region. I have passed Mora in 2010, 2014 and 2020, and during every visit it has marked the start of the journey to the wild North for me.

Tiveden National Park, Sweden
58°43'51.8"N 14°34'12.6"E

EXPLORE

Located just north of Mora, the Orsa Bear Park is a sanctuary for rescued bears, but also hosts other wildlife that is native to this part of Sweden. It provides a natural and spacious environment where you can observe the majestic Swedish wildlife.

Another highlight north of Mora is Hamra National Park, a serene mixture of bogs and forests. Ideal as a daytrip from Mora or as a stop along the way when you take the shorter itinerary that follows the E45.

Kaplangården, Mora
61°00’23.9”N 14°32’37.7”E

Fulufjället National Park, Sweden
61°38'15.6"N 12°42'34.0"E

140 km

SWEDEN

5 Fullufjället

Near the border with Norway in the centre of Sweden lies Fulufjället National Park, a pristine national park for nature enthusiasts and outdoor adventurers. This vast wilderness with impressive landscapes and diverse flora and fauna is home to the Njupeskär waterfall, Sweden's tallest one, which cascades down from a height of 93 metres. The hiking trails that wind through the bogs and ancient forests of Fulufjället offer plenty of opportunities to spot wildlife such as reindeer, lynx, and bears. It is the most southernly place where I have seen reindeer in Sweden, so keep your eyes on the road and the roadsides!

Njupeskär Waterfall, Fulufjället, Sweden
61°38'05.6"N 12°41'05.8"E

BN14

Reindeer next to road 311, Sweden
62°12'53.5"N 12°57'07.5"E

NORWAY

6 Sognefjord & Molden

As you travel westward and cross the border with Norway, the landscape gradually transforms into Norway's iconic mountainous terrain. Eventually, you will arrive at Sognefjord, the longest and deepest fjord in Norway. If weather permits and you love to hike, make the daytrip to the Molden. This moderate yet rewarding hike takes you to a summit that offers panoramic views of the surrounding fjords and valleys. This is one of the best places to capture the essence of Norway's majestic fjord landscapes.

Molden, Norway
61°20'13.0"N 7°18'04.6"E

NORWAY

7 Trollstigen via Ålesund

Norway features some of Europe's most spectacular roads to drive. One of them is the famous Trollstigen, which colours the cover of this book. From the town of Åndalsnes up to the mountain pass, the Trollstigen features 11 hairpin turns that span an elevation distance of 500 metres – few roads in Europe can compete with this stunning stretch of tarmac! Driving the Trollstigen is both a driver's and photographer's dream, offering countless opportunities to capture the striking scenery.

EXPLORE

A detour via Ålesund is very much worth the drive. Before you enter the town, make sure you drive to the Aksla Viewpoint that offers a magnificent view over the town, fjords, and sea.

Trollstigen, Norway
62°27'16.0"N 7°40'15.1"E

Aksla Viewpoint, Ålesund, Norway
62°28'27.4"N 6°09'50.5"E

NORWAY

8 Kristiansund via The Atlantic Ocean Road

As if the Trollstigen is not enough, there is another fantastic road coming up: the Atlantic Ocean Road, known as *Atlanterhavsveien* in Norwegian. This road stretches across a series of small islands, connecting archipelagos with striking bridges that seemingly blend with the surrounding ocean. The road winds and curves, offering spectacular views of the wild and untamed Norwegian Sea, which can wildly crash its waves against the rugged coastline and bridges. Kristiansund, at the end of the Atlantic Ocean Road, is a small maritime town with colourful houses and a lively harbour. Here you can continue to capture the essence of maritime life as fishing boats bob on the sparkling waters and seagulls soar above.

Atlanterhavsveien, Norway
63°01'00.6"N 7°20'53.3"E

460 km

SWEDEN

9 Östersund

The long and winding road continues back to Sweden, where you will reach Östersund. This will be the last large city until you reach Luleå, so make sure you replenish your supplies before you leave. Östersund is situated by Lake Storsjön, which is famous for Storsjöodjuret (*The Great-Lake Monster*). According to local folklore and tales, Storsjöodjuret is a large aquatic creature said to inhabit the depths of the lake. Stories of Storsjöodjuret date back centuries, and sightings and encounters have been reported over the years. The creature has become an intriguing part of the local culture and draws the attention of curious visitors who hope to catch a glimpse of the legendary monster.

Statue of Storsjöodjuret, Östersund, Sweden
63°10'12.3"N 14°36'37.4"E

270 km

SWEDEN

10 Skuleskogen

EXPLORE

If you take a short detour and follow road 90 southwards, you will soon arrive at the High Coast Bridge, a marvel of engineering that connects two parts of the Höga Kusten region.

The Höga Kusten, or High Coast, is one of the most significant post-glacial rebound areas on Earth, caused by the retreat of glaciers thousands of years ago. As the weight of the glaciers decreased after the Ice Age, the land gradually rose and continues to do so today at a rate of approximately 8-9 millimetres per year. This ongoing uplift has created high cliffs and exposed ancient seabeds, providing a glimpse into the geological history of the area. Skuleskogen National Park is a highlight of the High Coast. The unique geology has created a special natural scene of rocks, ancient forests, and dramatic coastal cliffs overlooking the sea.

Reindeer lichen is found abundantly in Skuleskogen National Park.

SWEDEN

11 Luleå & Gammelstad

Luleå is the capital of Norrbotten County, Sweden's most northernly county. Despite its modest size and remote location, Luleå is a modern city with a solid technical industry and one of Sweden's three universities of technology. As you walk along the promenade you will feel the lively atmosphere – time does not stand still here. Contrary to Luleå, the nearby Gammelstad transports you back in time. This UNESCO World Heritage site is known for its remarkably well-preserved church town, showcasing a collection of over 400 historic wooden buildings. Now it is an open-air museum, with the 15th-century Nederluleå Kyrka as its centrepiece.

Nederluleå Kyrka, Gammelstad, Sweden
65°38'44.5"N 22°01'41.9"E

250 km

SWEDEN

12 Jokkmokk & Laponia

EXPLORE

If you take road 94 and then road 374 towards Jokkmokk, you will have the opportunity to visit Storforsen, one of Europe's largest unregulated waterfalls. With a width of around 600 metres, the waterfall cascades over rugged rocks and creates a powerful display of rushing water.

Just after crossing the magic Arctic Circle at a latitude of 66°33′49.5″N, you will arrive in Jokkmokk, the cultural and historical hub of the Sami, the reindeer-herding people of Lapland. Spread to the north and west of Jokkmokk lies Laponia, a vast wilderness and the largest area on Earth that is still cultivated by indigenous people – the Sami in this case. Where the national parks of Muddus and Stora Sjöfallet are accessible for day hikes, the other two national parks Sarek and Padjelanta cannot be explored in one day since the entrance of the park lies far away from public roads. I have stood of the border of Sarek after a long hike, catching only a glimpse of the remoteness ahead of me. This is where nature really remains untouched.

Muddus, Laponia, Sweden
67°02'15.4"N 20°03'07.5"E

EXPLORE

In Jokkmokk you can learn about the Sami culture and Arctic environment in the Ájtte Museum, which I highly recommend visiting. It also has a lot of quality handicrafts and local delicacies on offer, which will be a perfect opportunity to take home some authentic souvenirs.

The road to Sarek, Laponia, Sweden
67°06'46.2"N 18°26'20.5"E

260 km

SWEDEN

13 Abisko

EXPLORE

Visit the Kiruna Mine, which is one of the largest underground iron ore mines in the world. An interesting fact is that due to subsidence caused by mining, they are now moving the city of Kiruna to a new site about three kilometres from the current town centre.

Abisko is a small settlement at the Torneträsk lake. Although a serene setting between the imposing mountains, this area has a harsh climate, of which the short full-grown birch trees are a proof. Summers are very short and when I visited the Torneträsk in May, large patches of ice were still present on the lake's surface. At Abisko, the iconic Kungsleden (King's Trail) starts or ends its 440 kilometres through Sweden's remote nature. For a day hike, a popular segment is the section from Abisko to the south towards the lake Abiskojaure and back. This trail is well-marked and showcases the raw beauty of Swedish Lapland.

Kungsleden to Abiskojaure,
Abisko, Sweden
68°18'42.5"N 18°41'00.0"E

NORWAY

14 Lofoten

As soon as the Lofoten archipelago appears on the horizon, you will realise that you have come to one of the most stunning places on Earth. I often nickname it *Switzerland by the Sea* given the landscape full of mountains that soar over 1000 metres above the ocean. Lofoten is also known for its traditional fishing industry, and stockfish in particular. The little town of Svolvær is a good starting place for your exploration of Lofoten, and one of the best places to explore the world of stockfish. This dried and preserved cod, traditionally air-dried on wooden racks, has been prepared here for over a thousand years. The penetrating smell around the wooden racks may or may not steal your appetite, but stockfish is a highly sought-after delicacy in some countries!

View near Knutstad, Lofoten, Norway
68°16'36.5"N 13°57'54.2"E

Henningsvær, Lofoten, Norway
68°09'04.9"N 14°11'50.2"E

‘I often nickname Lofoten *Switzerland by the Sea*, given the landscape full of mountains that soar over 1000 metres above the ocean’

Svolvær, Lofoten, Norway
68°14’03.7”N 14°34’23.9”E

The last 1000 kilometres of this road trip, from Lofoten to the North Cape, are the grand finale and a real pleasure to drive, observe, feel, smell, and photograph. Once we approach the sea near Narvik, we immediately notice the change in landscape as we are leaving behind the harsh inland climate. I am glad to see some other trees than miniature birches after being out in Abisko National Park for a few days.

I am also happy to see the bright-blue sky and sun, because I hope to catch the Midnight Sun anywhere during the next couple of days. All hotels feature blackout curtains here, but at 11 p.m. it still feels like we are going to sleep in the late afternoon.

390

NORWAY

15 Lyngen

Following the E6 in northern direction for a few hours, you will arrive at one of the most beautiful fjords of the whole of Norway. Lyngen is a stunning fjord located in Troms County, which stretches approximately 82 kilometres to the open sea. The Lyngen Alps, with their majestic peaks and glaciers, provide a dramatic backdrop to the fjord. The region is a paradise for nature enthusiasts and adventure seekers, with its pristine wilderness and abundance of wildlife. And it has been one of the most serene settings for a stove-prepared dinner on all my travels, just next to the road!

Lyngen, Norway
69°25'53.6"N 20°16'46.1"E

Lyngen, Norway
69°25'55.0"N 20°16'45.0"E

270 km

NORWAY

16 Alta

Just before you head off to the most northernly point of mainland Europe, a surprise awaits in Alta. This town is not only nestled amidst wild landscapes, but it is also the home of ancient rock carvings, known as the Alta Rock Art. These carvings date back thousands of years and are recognised as a UNESCO World Heritage site. The carvings depict scenes from daily life, animals, and symbols, providing insights into the culture and beliefs of prehistoric communities. The idea that ancient people have lived here and even had the ability to create these markings is very fascinating, and a great cultural counterpart to the unearthly eye-catching landscapes of Northern Norway.

Rock art of Alta, Norway
69°57'05.7"N 23°11'40.1"E

Reindeer on the E6 to Alta, Norway
69°52'44.0"N 21°58'28.7"E

'Continuing the E69, you will reach
the legendary North Cape,
a majestic cliff rising over 300 metres
above the Arctic Ocean'

Near the North Cape, Magerøya, Norway
71°08'36.9"N 25°44'39.2"E

240 km

NORWAY

17 The North Cape

On the final stretch to reach the North Cape, the landscape transforms into an Arctic tundra. The North Cape Tunnel allows you to pass beneath the sea to reach the island of Magerøya, after which you arrive in Honningsvåg, the northernmost town in Norway. Here, you will be greeted by a lively coastal setting and a bustling atmosphere, which is partly due to the frequent visits of the famous Hurtigruten cruise ships. Continuing the E69, you will reach the legendary North Cape, a majestic cliff rising over 300 metres above the Arctic Ocean. The North Cape is an iconic landmark and considered the northernmost point of mainland Europe. In this wild and rough environment, the sun never sets in summer. The golden glow over the landscape of the Midnight Sun creates an otherworldly ambiance that is the perfect end of this epic road trip.

The North Cape, Magerøya, Norway
71°10'15.3"N 25°46'59.0"E

Personal notes

Scandinavia has always been one of my favourite destinations. The wild landscapes and raw beauty, and particularly the emptiness of some regions is simply enchanting. Although I do not like cold wind, rain and mosquitoes, the weather has been very generous to me throughout my travels in 2010, 2014, 2020 and 2021. I have crossed the Arctic Circle from South to North three times, always in good weather. During my most recent trip in August and September 2021, we have had exceptionally sunny days, which made for an unforgettable wild camping experience with the rooftop tent on my Subaru Forester. But regardless of the weather, Scandinavia is one of the best destinations for nature lovers – which is exactly why I keep coming back.

On the top of the Molden,
Sognefjord, Norway
61°20'42.5"N 7°18'58.5"E

Rovinj, Croatia
45°04'34.0"N 13°38'14.9"E

Fifteen fantastic **photographic viewpoints**

Some places in Europe are so photogenic that virtually *everyone* will grab their camera. As a travel photographer I have always been on the lookout for gorgeous locations and typically spend quite some time preparing for a trip, so I know where to go when I have arrived in the region. Here I will share some of my favourites with you. Whether you like to photograph or not, the fantastic view at the locations below will make a lasting impression on you.

1 **Meteora** | Greece – 39°43'15.7"N 21°38'01.4"E
2 **Neist Point** | **Isle of Skye** | Scotland – 57°25'49.4"N 6°46'59.5"W
3 **Monte Titano** | Republic of San Marino – 43°55'58.2"N 12°27'06.2"E
4 **Kop van Zuid** | **Rotterdam** | The Netherlands – 51°54'11.4"N 4°29'09.7"E
5 **Piva Lake** | Montenegro – 43°10'26.7"N 18°51'29.6"E
6 **Rovinj** | Croatia – 45°04'49.6"N 13°38'08.1"E
7 **Berdorf** | Luxembourg – 49°49'55.6"N 6°20'40.8"E
8 **Ålesund** | Norway – 62°28'27.3"N 6°09'50.4"E
9 **Cliffs of Moher** | Ireland – 52°58'38.9"N 9°25'33.9"W
10 **Transfăgărășan** | Romania – 45°36'29.4"N 24°37'02.1"E
11 **Plitvice Lakes National Park** | Croatia – 44°52'33.2"N 15°35'55.4"E
12 **Puy Mary** | France – 45°06'41.1"N 2°40'25.7"E
13 **Lyngen** | Norway – 69°25'55.0"N 20°16'45.0"E
14 **Sintra-Cascais Coast** | Portugal – 38°46'43.6"N 9°29'53.0"W
15 **Râpa Roșie** | Sebeș | Romania – 45°59'08.4"N 23°35'30.5"E

Vitsa, Greece
39°52'24.9"N 20°44'34.7"E

6

AROUND THE ADRIATIC

A trip through Europe's **unforgettable paradise**

The grand finale of this book is a journey through Europe's best-kept secret: the Balkans. Stretching all the way from Italy via Slovenia to Greece, this 3000-kilometres long road trip takes you through eight countries and a multitude of cultural encounters. The roads close to the Adriatic Sea offer stunning coastal views, while the lakes of Croatia's Plitvice and Krka and the roads and hiking trails of inland Montenegro will surely have a lasting impression on even the seasoned road trip travellers.

More to the South, Albania shows a mixture of mountain landscapes and cultural history – especially the well-preserved Ottoman towns of Berat and Gjirokastër. Then, nearing the edge of our continent, you enter Greece. Mainland Greece is home to snowy mountains, extraordinary monasteries, rough coastal landscapes, and ancient ruins, just to name a few highlights. The one destination in Europe that I would recommend everyone to visit is Meteora in Greece, a series of monasteries set in an unearthly beautiful scenery which colours the last pages of this book.

This is a road trip like it is meant to be. Full of nature, culture, culinary experiences and full of adventure. Enjoy your journey around the Adriatic Sea and through the Balkans, it will not get any better than this.

ITALY

REPUBLIC OF SAN MARINO

SLOVENIA

CROATIA

BOSNIA & HERZEGOVINA

MONTENEGRO

ALBANIA

GREECE

Ville di Corsano, Italy
43°13'20.2"N 11°20'36.0"E

THE COMPLETE ROUTE

A trip trough Europe's **unforgettable paradise**

Total length
3000 km

Countries
Italy | Republic of San Marino | Slovenia
Croatia | Bosnia & Herzegovina
Montenegro | Albania | Greece

Time
4-5 weeks

Best season
September to June. Summers tend to be (too) hot.

Destinations
1 **Province of Siena**
2 **San Marino** – 200 km
3 **Verona** – 290 km
4 **Ljubljana** – 340 km
5 **Rovinj** – 180 km
6 **Adriatic Highway** – 270 km
7 **Split** via **Zadar** – 220 km
8 **Dubrovnik** – 230 km
9 **Mostar** – 140 km
10 **Sarajevo** – 120 km
11 **Durmitor via Piva** – 170 km
12 **North Albanian Alps** – 180 km
13 **Berat & Gjirokastër** – 410 km
14 **Pindos Mountains** – 110 km
15 **Meteora** – 140 km

Balance*
Nature ●●●●
Culture ●●●●●
Culinary ●●●●●

* (max 5 dots)

SHORTER ROUTES

A culinary circle around the **Adriatic**

Total length
1550 km

Time
2 weeks

Destinations
3 | 4 | 5 | 6 | 7 | 8

Balance
Nature ●●●●
Culture ●●●
Culinary ●●●●●

Cities of the **Southeast**

Total length
1650 km

Time
2 weeks

Destinations
4 | 5 | 7 | 8 | 9 | 10

Balance
Nature ●●●●
Culture ●●●
Culinary ●●●●

Best of the **Balkan Mountains**

Total length
1850 km

Time
2-3 weeks

Destinations
11 | 12 | 13 | 14 | 15

Balance
Nature ●●●●
Culture ●●●
Culinary ●●●

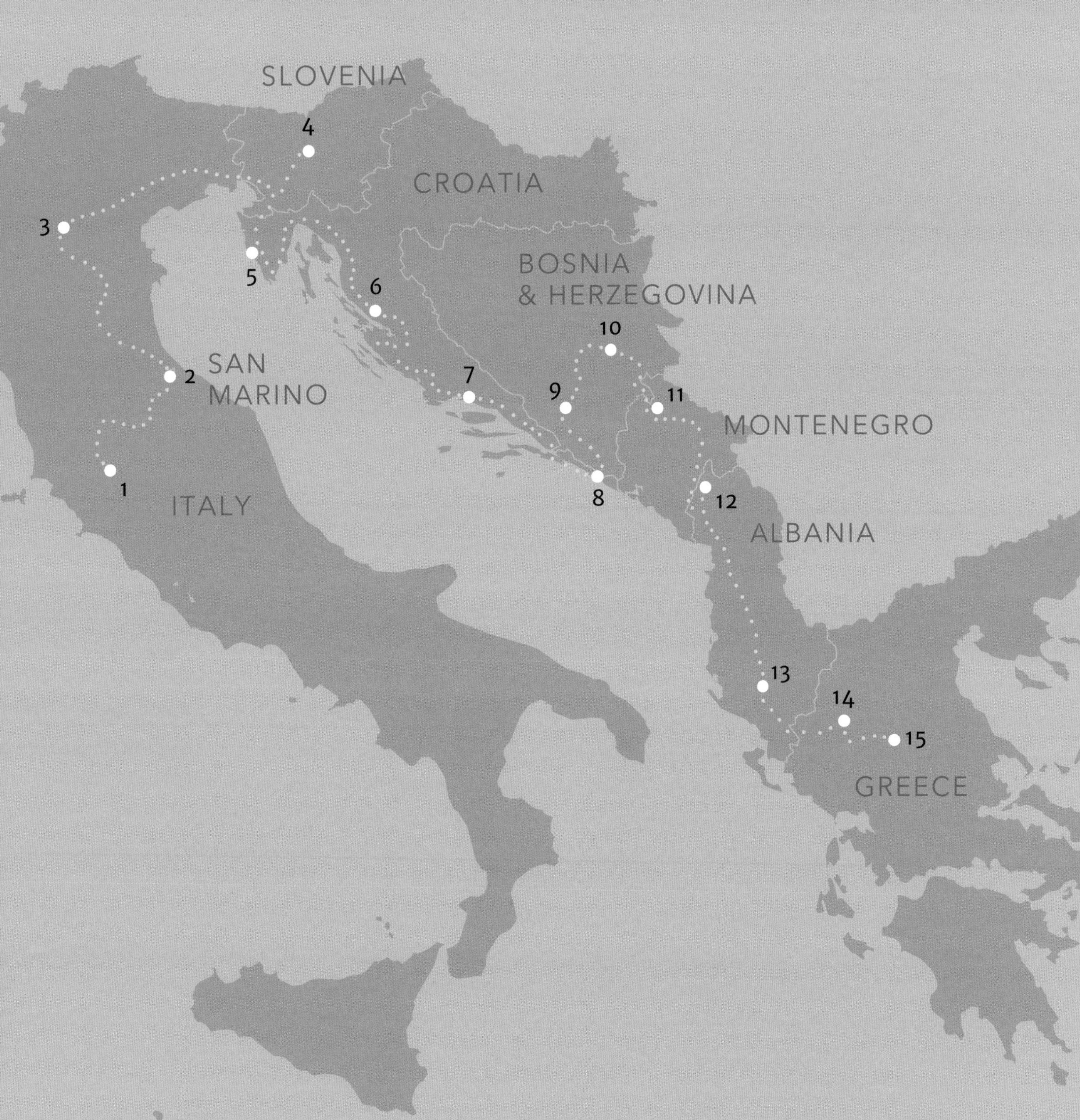
SLOVENIA
4
CROATIA
3
5
BOSNIA
& HERZEGOVINA
6
10
SAN
MARINO
2
7
9
11
MONTENEGRO
1
ITALY
8
12
ALBANIA
13
14
15
GREECE

Outside an abandoned house near San Gimignano, this lizard observes every movement of my camera.

ITALY

1 Province of Siena

Nestled in the heart of Tuscany, the Province of Siena offers a blend of picturesque landscapes, historical charm, and famous wines, making it a paradise for photographers and wine enthusiasts alike. With its rolling hills, medieval towns, and vineyard-covered valleys, Siena is a masterpiece waiting to be captured through the lens or tasted by the glass. Next to the typical Tuscan landscapes that can be found in the Val d'Orcia, I particularly like San Gimignano. This little town is sometimes nicknamed *Medieval Manhattan* due to the various towers that form the skyline.

EXPLORE

Visit the hilltop fortress Montalcino, which is known for its full-bodied Brunello di Montalcino that can be tasted everywhere in the town.

Cypress Road, Val d'Orcia, Italy
43°01'38.4"N 11°46'31.4"E

Crete Senesi, Tuscany, Italy
43°11'56.5"N 11°35'18.8"E

REPUBLIC
OF SAN MARINO

2 San Marino

On approaching the Republic of San Marino – one of Europe's fascinating microstates – you immediately understand why a fortress was built here. The castle on top of Monte Titano provides gorgeous views over the surrounding lands. Though it was almost completely quiet when I visited San Marino in February, I can imagine that it is a popular place in summer, so best if you avoid the peak of the holiday season. Go up early in the morning or late in the afternoon when the sun's side lighting emphasises the texture and depth of the landscape around you.

Prima Torre, Monte Titano, San Marino
43°56'04.7"N 12°27'00.3"E

View from Monte Titano, San Marino
43°55'58.2"N 12°27'06.2"E

EXPLORE

The Dolomites are only 150 kilometres away from Verona. If you want to explore a spectacular part the Southern Alps, then go to the Dolomiti di Brenta mountain range, a fantastic place to hike and inhale fresh mountain air.

Near Cascata di Vallesinella,
Dolomiti di Brenta, Italy
46°12'25.0"N 10°52'10.3"E

290 km

ITALY

3 Verona

Apart from its detailed architecture and romantic setting by the river Adige, Verona also has one of the best-preserved Roman amphitheatres in the world, the Verona Arena, which is still used for opera performances today. Verona is also home of the excellent Amarone wines, a strong and rich red wine of a blend of grapes that is crafted by a unique drying and fermentation process. Of all the famous Italian wines, this is my preferred one and worth to try when you are in the region. But this is not a wine to drink without a good meal, so take a tasty risotto on the side, which also comes from this region.

Verona, Italy
45°26’41.3”N 11°00’07.7”E

340 km

SLOVENIA

4 Ljubljana

EXPLORE

Close to Ljubljana lies a picturesque landscape scene, Lake Bled. Beautifully set on the foot of the Alps and protected Triglav National Park with gondolas dotted across the lake, few scenes in Europe are more romantic than this one. Avoid the peak of summer, as more people have discovered this destination in recent years.

Often regarded as the greenest city in Europe, Ljubljana is known for its commitment to environmental sustainability and its dedication to preserving its natural surroundings. The city centre is a pedestrian-friendly haven, with its historic streets lined with lush green trees, flower-filled parks, and many outdoor cafes. Ljubljana Castle proudly stands atop Castle Hill, offering panoramic views of the city and the green landscapes that surround it.

180 km

CROATIA

5 Rovinj

Situated on the Adriatic Sea, Rovinj is a lovely medieval town on the Croatian peninsula Istria. It has a rich cultural heritage influenced by various civilizations, including Roman, Venetian, and Austro-Hungarian. The Old Town consists of a labyrinth of narrow cobblestone streets, charming squares, and colourful buildings. It is a popular tourist destination, so you will not feel alone and there are plenty of cafés, restaurants, and boutiques to keep you busy throughout the day. Despite its popularity and occasional crowdedness, Rovinj is too photogenic to not include on this road trip!

EXPLORE

Also famous is the well-preserved amphitheatre of Pula in the southern tip of Istria. The town itself is interesting to explore, even more so because of its contrast in atmosphere compared to Rovinj.

View from Ljubljanski grad, Ljubljana, Slovenia
46°02'55.9"N 14°30'28.2"E

Rovinj, Croatia
45°04'49.6"N 13°38'08.1"E

Close to Rovinj lies Bale, also a medieval village but much smaller and quieter than Rovinj. I am staying over in this village for two nights and soon discover that Bale is known for its olive oil production.

In Istria, people drink olive oil by the glass, pour it over their ice-creams (yes, that is very tasty indeed!), and use it as body or hair oil. On the second morning of my stay in June 2013, I have planned an olive oil tasting session at the small, family-owned olive oil mill Grubić. After a private tour and three small shots of completely different kinds of olive oil, I am totally impressed and stuff my car with more bottles than I should try to squeeze in the last spaces of the fully packed car.

Since that tasting session I use this cold-pressed delicacy for just about everything! And this particular one from Bale has become a special treat for me, so I even returned in 2022 for new bottles of this liquid gold.

Olive tree near Bale, Croatia
45°02'32.0"N 13°45'05.1"E

270 km

CROATIA

6 Adriatic Highway

EXPLORE

Explore Paklenica National Park. With its rugged limestone canyons and towering cliffs, it is no wonder that rock climbing is a popular activity here. The Paklenica climbing area is one of the best-managed in Europe and offers routes for all climbing levels. For those that do not want to defy gravity, the National Park offers walking trails and various places where you can take a refreshing swim in the Velika Paklenica River.

The Adriatic Highway, also known as the Jadranska Magistrala, is the scenic E65 that spans along the eastern Adriatic coastline. Starting from the northern border of Croatia and winding its way southwards, it offers fantastic views of the turquoise waters of the Adriatic Sea, and you will encounter numerous charming villages and towns along the way. The most spectacular stretch of road is between Senj and Starigrad, with some options to take a side road up the mountains for a higher viewpoint. Best done in sunny weather, which will give you the ultimate summer travelling feeling, even in winter!

Jadranska Magistrala (E65), Croatia
44°31'04.3"N 15°05'15.8"E

EXPLORE

Make a day trip to the world-famous Plitvice Lakes National Park. Though the number of visitors coming to this paradise landscape is truly absurd, you can avoid a large part of the crowd by taking one of the longer walking routes. Declared as one of the world wonders, Plitvice Lakes National Parks offers one of the most beautiful natural landscapes in Europe and is a must-see if you have not been there yet.

Near Supljara Cave, Plitvička Jezera, Croatia
44°53'59.7"N 15°36'41.9"E

Plitvička Jezera (Plitvice Lakes National Park), Croatia
44°53'41.3"N 15°36'34.3"E

220 km

CROATIA

7 Split via Zadar

Zadar has a long and varied multi-cultural history, which is still visible today by the Roman ruins, medieval churches, and narrow cobblestone streets that colour the Old Town. It is a perfect place for lunch or an overnight stop before you travel on to Split. Once you arrive in Split, you will experience that this is a worldly city unlike the ones you have seen so far in Croatia. Split is the second-largest city in Croatia and holds strategic importance as a major port city on the eastern Adriatic coast. It is also known for its rich historical heritage, including the Diocletian's Palace. With a bustling tourism industry, the many fancy bars and restaurants along the marina will give even the seasoned city visitor a choice overload.

EXPLORE

In Zadar, be sure to visit the fascinating Sea Organ along the waterfront, which is a large experimental instrument that produces music through the waves of the sea.

Sea Organ, Zadar, Croatia
44°07'03.3"N 15°13'10.5"E

'The many fancy bars and restaurants along the marina will give even the seasoned city visitor a choice overload'

Split, Croatia
43°30'14.2"N 16°25'46.4"E

EXPLORE

Between Zadar and Split lies Krka National Park, which somewhat resembles Plitvice Lakes National Park. Krka is much smaller in size though, and the flora is less abundant than in Plitvice. But the panoramic views from higher up are not inferior to those of its famous larger brother!

Krka, Croatia
43°48'19.9"N 15°57'58.2"E

230 km

CROATIA

8 Dubrovnik

EXPLORE

Biokovo is a majestic mountain range that is part of the Dinaric Alps. The roads and hiking trails that go up in the mountains offer outstanding views of the Adriatic Sea and the surrounding islands.

Before July 2022, reaching one of Croatia's most gorgeous cities and famous ports required two non-Schengen border crossings in roughly ten kilometres. Now you can take the Pelješac Bridge instead, which brings you to the last part of Croatia's spectacular Adriatic coastline without crossing Bosnia & Herzegovina. Upon entering Dubrovnik, you will cross another spectacular bridge, Franjo Tuđman, which is a beautiful photographic location during the blue hour. The city itself has an historic old town that is encircled by ancient walls. The city has a stunning setting on the Dalmatian coast, which is best viewed from locations higher up, such as Fort Imperial, which also features an interesting war museum.

Dubrovnik, Croatia
42°40'11.6"N 18°04'37.5"E

EXPLORE

Hvar is a great additional stop along the way if you want to explore the Dalmatian islands. Take the ferry from Drvenik, which brings you to the edge of Hvar in about half an hour. From there it is still quite a drive to the main city on Hvar (with the same name), so be sure that you start your return drive soon enough to catch the last ferry to mainland Croatia. Hvar also has many quiet beaches, where you can dive into the crystal-clear Adriatic Sea.

Hvar, Croatia
43°07'21.5"N 17°11'45.9"E

Mostar, Bosnia & Herzegovina
43°20'07.9"N 17°48'56.5"E

140 km

BOSNIA &
HERZEGOVINA

9 Mostar

EXPLORE

I recommend visiting Muslibegović House, an open-air museum which takes you back to the Ottoman Empire and gives you a good impression of life during this period in history.

About 140 kilometres from Dubrovnik lies Mostar, an historical city that is particularly known for its iconic Stari Most (Old Bridge) that spans the Neretva River. Mostar was an important trading centre during the Ottoman period, and its architecture, cuisine, and traditions reflect this rich heritage. Mostar's recent history is marred by the Bosnian War (1992-1995), during which the city faced significant destruction, including the deliberate destruction of the Old Bridge in 1993. After the war, efforts were made to reconstruct the bridge using traditional techniques and materials. The result has become a photogenic symbol of resilience and reconciliation.

Muslibegović House, Mostar,
Bosnia & Herzegovina
43°20'30.5"N 17°48'59.3"E

BOSNIA & HERZEGOVINA

10 Sarajevo

Sarajevo, the capital of Bosnia & Herzegovina, beautifully blends East and West and seamlessly merges different cultures, religions, and architectural styles. The city is divided by the Miljacka River, with the eastern part predominantly inhabited by Bosniaks and the western part by Bosnian Croats and Serbs, symbolising the historical and cultural division. Despite its complex history, Sarajevo embraces a remarkably friendly and welcoming atmosphere. Its residents take pride in their multicultural identity and are known for their warm hospitality. But like Mostar, Sarajevo also has its scars of the Bosnian War. Numerous war memorials and sites, including the Sarajevo Roses, mark the tragic events that unfolded during the conflict.

Sarajevo, Bosnia & Herzegovina
43°51'55.7"N 18°26'23.4"E

It is a warm and sunny morning in Sarajevo, and I have planned a visit to the Gazi Husrev-beg Mosque in the heart of the city. Upon arrival in the garden surrounding the mosque, I am greeted by a man dressed casually in a pair of jeans and leather jacket. He firmly shakes hands and starts to talk about the mosque, its history, and his view on religion.

To him, there are no 'right' or 'wrong' religions, and he explains that many religions share the same foundations. The Bosnians seem to understand this concept very well. Once inside the mosque, marvelling at the beautiful interior, my guide explains that he is the Imam of this mosque, and he offers to sing a call to prayer. A fantastic voice echoes through the building, which leaves me speechless.

This intriguing tour and the philosophic talks with the Imam changed my view on the concept of religion forever – in a very positive way.

Gazi Husrev-beg Mosque, Sarajevo,
Bosnia & Herzegovina
43°51'33.3"N 18°25'44.7"E

'Once you are surrounded by the mountains,
the dense, dark forests, and
pitch-black lakes, you will understand
why the name of this country
is Crna Gora, meaning *Black Mountain*'

170 km

MONTENEGRO

11 Durmitor via Piva

The route from Sarajevo to Durmitor is an exciting road to drive. The gorgeous E762 leads through countless short tunnels and offers fantastic views over the water deep down in the canyon below, all the way until you reach the triple intersection where the water arms of Piva Lake join. From there you drive up towards Durmitor following the P14, which offers brilliant views over Piva Lake. As the road continues high above the canyon, you will see the landscape of Durmitor National Park unfolding. This is an excellent destination for hikers, with Crno Jerezo being a good place to lace up your hiking shoes. Once you are surrounded by the mountains, the dense, dark forests, and pitch-black lakes, you will understand why the name of this country is Crna Gora, meaning *Black Mountain*.

EXPLORE

Hum Border Crossing between Bosnia & Herzegovina and Montenegro is the most adventurous border crossing you will encounter on your trip through the Balkans. Despite its raw appearance with a shaky wooden bridge, border control is not much different from other crossings, fortunately, though it can be busy at times.

Piva Lake, Montenegro
43°10'26.7"N 18°51'29.6"E

40

SH20 near Rrapshë, Albania
42°24'52.4"N 19°29'53.3"E

Crno Jezero, Montenegro
43°08'48.4"N 19°05'46.6"E

EXPLORE

On your way to Albania, you can plan additional stops in Biogradska National Park – an attractive lake with dense forests surrounding it – and Montenegro's capital Podgorica. Though Podgorica might not show the historical grandeur of many other European capitals, it does give a true travellers' experience of visiting a capital with hardly any tourists.

ALBANIA

12 North Albanian Alps

Albania has an almost mythical atmosphere due to its rough landscape, historical Ottoman towns, unique language, and the many thousands of bunkers that are spread out across the country. These bunkers originate from the communist regime that lasted until 1985, and their number is estimated to be at least 173,000. This makes it impossible to ignore them, even in seemingly remote landscapes like the North Albanian Alps. This rough landscape of peaks and steep slopes is nicknamed *Accursed Mountains*, locally also known as Bjeshkët e Nëmuna, which makes you wonder what happens in these mountains. But whether you are driving the outstanding scenic road SH20 or go up SH21 to start a day hike in the mountains, the devil that supposedly escaped from hell is already long gone.

Rrapsh Serpentine (SH20), Albania
42°24'55.0"N 19°30'11.9"E

410 km

ALBANIA

13 Berat & Gjirokastër

Berat, *The City of a Thousand Windows*, shows a unique mix of Byzantine and Ottoman influences. Traditional Ottoman houses line the hillsides and create a picturesque scene with their whitewashed walls, wooden balconies, and rows of countless windows. After a little climb up the hill, you will reach Berat Castle, or Kalaja e Beratit in Albanian, which dates back to the 4th century BC and has witnessed the rise and fall of different civilizations. Gjirokastër, on the other hand, is famous for its well-preserved Ottoman stone houses. You can also climb up here: Gjirokastër Fortress and its wide views over the surrounding lands are worth every step. Although Berat and Gjirokastër have their similarities and are both UNESCO World Heritage Sites, it is interesting to visit both cities since they breathe a different atmosphere – something that is difficult to describe on paper.

Berat, Albania
40°42'08.1"N 19°56'54.2"E

Gjirokastër, Albania
40°04'27.1"N 20°08'27.1"E

View from Panorama Llogara (SH8), Albania
40°11'17.5"N 19°35'57.9"E

EXPLORE

The Blue Eye (Syri i Kaltër in Albanian) is a natural phenomenon near the village of Muzinë. It is a spring from a deep underground source of water that forms a bright blue pool surrounded by lush green vegetation. The seemingly bottomless pool of crystal-clear water resembles an eye in the middle of a dense forest.

Syri i Kaltër (The Blue Eye), Albania
42°21'53.7"N 19°44'49.6"E

GREECE

14 Pindos Mountains

Nearing the southern end of the Balkans, you arrive in Greece. Where most people only know Greece from Athens and the various touristic islands, the true surprises are found inland, in Northern Greece. One of them is Pindos (or Pindus), a pristine mountain range north of Ioannina. It offers several well-established trails that lead through diverse landscapes, including alpine meadows, deep gorges, and rugged peaks. One notable trail is the Vikos Gorge Trail, which takes you through the spectacular Vikos Gorge, supposedly the deepest gorge in the world relative to its width.

EXPLORE

The town of Monodendri, located in the Zagori region of the Pindos Mountains, is a small village that serves as a gateway to the natural wonders of the area. It features traditional stone houses, cobbled streets, and a laid-back atmosphere that exudes a sense of timeless beauty.

Near Papingo, Pindos Mountains, Greece
39°57'40.2"N 20°42'11.4"E

140 km

GREECE

15 Meteora

Spoiler: no adjectives and superlatives in the description of Meteora do justice to this unearthly beautiful scenery. The name Meteora means *suspended in the air*, which perfectly captures the essence of this unique place. Towering sandstone pillars rise abruptly from the surrounding plain, creating a scene that seems almost otherworldly. Perched atop these towering rocks are ancient monasteries that were constructed by monks seeking isolation and spiritual seclusion, and they blend harmoniously with the natural surroundings. Meteora is a place where geology meets architecture in an absolutely stunning setting. Though best visited in soft sunlight or during the blue hour, Meteora will make a lasting impression on everyone, anytime of the day, anytime of the year.

The Holy Monastery of Saint Nicholas
Anapafsas, Meteora, Greece
39°43'15.6"N 21°38'01.8"E

'The name Meteora means
suspended in the air, which perfectly captures
the essence of this unique place'

Kastraki, Greece
39°42'59.1"N 21°37'26.6"E

Monastery of Varlaam, Meteora, Greece
39°43'30.2"N 21°37'48.4"E

Ohrid, North Macedonia
41°06'39.1"N 20°47'18.5"E

Personal notes

The road trip described here is composed based on my travels to the Balkans and Italy in 2013, 2015, 2016, the winter of 2018/2019, and 2022. No other region in Europe shows so much variation in culture and nature in such a small geographic area as the Balkans. With so much on offer, I am surprised to see that still few people make the drive through this fantastic part of Europe, but that definitely adds to its charm. The Balkans offer the perfect blend of unforgettable landscapes, historical architecture, thrilling outdoor adventures, relaxing accommodation, and culinary delights. Unfortunately, not all countries of the Balkans that I favour could be covered in the 256 pages of this book. But if you are on your way back from Greece and want to drive a different route to the North, I invite you to visit at least North Macedonia, which also features some highlights of the Balkans such as the very romantic Lake Ohrid and the wild Mavrovo National Park.

Gorgeous roads
to drive in Europe

Europe boasts some winding and wild roads to drive! Below you will find a list of roads or stretches of road that you will be able to drive when following the road trips in this book. They are scenic highlights and offer brilliant views of the surrounding landscapes. Some boost your adrenaline with their sharp hairpin turns, others seem to disappear into infinity on the distant horizon. One thing all these roads have in common: they are a proven recipe for the ultimate road trip experience.

- **Transfăgărășan (DN7C)** | Romania
- **Trollstigen (FV63)** | Norway
- **SH20** between **Lake Skadar** & **Tamarë** | Albania
- **E69** to the **North Cape** | Norway
- **M18 & P14** between **Hum** & **Žabljak** | Montenegro
- **R335** through **Mweelrea** & **Doo Lough Region** | Ireland
- **Jadranska Magistrala (E65)** between **Senj** & **Starigrad** | Croatia
- **Ex-208** | **Extremadura** | Spain
- **E92** between **Koridallos** & **Megali Kerasia** | Greece
- **A855** | **Isle of Skye** | **Scotland** | UK
- **M20** & **M18** between **Čemerno** & **Vučevo** | Bosnia & Herzegovina
- **E10** between **Kiruna** & **Å** | Sweden & Norway
- **DN18** between **Şesuri** & **Borșa** | Romania
- **Atlanterhavsveien (Atlantic Ocean Road)** | Norway
- **SH8** between **Orikum** & **Himarë** | Albania
- **D17** & **D680** around **Pas de Peyrol** | France
- **Sky Road** | **County Galway** | Ireland

On the SH8
to Dhërmi, Albania
40°11'26.6"N 19°36'33.1"E

Biserica Sfânta Treime, Sighişoara, Romania
46°13'18.0"N 24°47'39.4"E

Enjoying a walk through
the North Sea dunes.

About **the author**

Ever since I got the keys of my first car – a silver Subaru Impreza from 2001 – I have felt a sense of freedom and the urge to explore Europe. On that sunny day in late July 2008, when I was still studying at Delft University of Technology, I immediately started making plans on what to do with those keys to freedom after my graduation, and the idea to make road trips through Europe was born. I had no idea of the spectacular adventures and roads that would literally lie ahead of me.

The first serious road trip took place in May 2010, when my partner Martijn and I took a month off from our first jobs and packed the car for a journey to the North. The 9500-kilometres trip from the Netherlands to the North Cape was such a wonderful adventure! It became clear that road trips fitted perfectly to our way our travelling. Many more journeys came up, including longer trips to the UK in 2011, France and the Iberian Peninsula in 2012, a journey to the Black Sea and particularly Romania in 2013, and exploring the northeast and east of Europe in 2014. On that trip in 2014, when we encountered a truck from Azerbaijan in Moldova, we came up with the bizarre idea to make a journey all the way to Baku at the Caspian Sea in 2015. Plans became reality, and so we found ourselves completing the epic 14,500-kilometres adventure of a lifetime through 20 countries in October 2015. It was a journey of extremes, of fantastic landscapes, of *remoteness*, of exploration, of countless colours and flavours, and one of resilience at times. But it was worth every kilometre.

Continuing our curiosity for exploration, we made a trip to Italy, Malta, and Cyprus in 2016, and finally explored the winter wonderland of Iceland in 2017, the last of the 50 European countries to cover in just 7 years. After that we kept (re)exploring Europe, and even drove from the Netherlands to the Sahara and back in that old Subaru, just because we loved it. And we both still do.

‘I had no idea of the spectacular adventures and roads that would literally lie ahead of me’

In 2018 I welcomed a new kid on the block: a Subaru Forester from 2011. After 10 years of road trip adventures and driving through 50 countries, the Impreza became worn and I wanted to have a bit more flexibility to drive offroad while still having a representative car to commute to my clients. So the Forester became the new big (but younger) brother to our Impreza, who managed to reach an impressive 493,510 kilometres in the end! Both its retirement and the welcoming of the golden retriever Alex to my home marked the start of a transition. Since a couple of years, I focus on exploring a region in more detail, rather than covering a larger distance. My new partner and travel companion Rainier has joined Alex and me on these journeys since 2021. The three of us are sold to the concept of travelling with a rooftop tent and camping out in the wild. Life does not get any better when you are warming yourself around a cosy campfire while watching the day turning to night amidst Europe’s gorgeous landscapes.

On every journey and in every European country, a camera has joined me on the road – most often a DSLR from Nikon but also a mirrorless Leica accompanied me in recent years. I have been photographing actively since 2005 and during my time at university I have had the opportunity to develop myself as an all-round freelance photographer. My work has ranged from capturing rocket launches to wedding ceremonies and from promotional photoshoots to real estate. Since 2010 I have also given workshops, lectures, and training on photography, because I love to share both my technical knowledge and artistic side on camera handling, composition, lighting, and editing imagery.

This love for combining creativity with technology is also reflected in my work in the geospatial domain, where I can combine design, image editing, cartography, writing and my passion for geography and the Earth – all these elements are also reflected in *On the Road in Europe*. By capturing and sharing the map of Europe in colourful photographs, I hope to inspire you to hit the road and explore as well!

Fanad Head, Ireland
55°16'36.5"N 7°38'00.7"W

Flying along from Texel to Den Helder, the Netherlands
52°59'32.5"N 4°47'18.0"E

Acknowledgements

First and foremost, thanks go to the three men that have accompanied me in life and on the road.

In chronological order, thank you papa, for taking me on so many miniature road trips when I was a child. I remember going on an expedition to watch the solar eclipse in August 1999 together. Examining maps and weather forecasts, we were debating where to go – Normandy or Saarbrücken? Regardless the outcome and the fact that it was cloudy when the actual eclipse moment was there, I really enjoyed being on the road with you. Not only on this trip, but on all our adventures, big and small. I admire how you still explore Europe together with mama. The two of you have been and still are an inspiration on how to spend your retirement exploring Europe.

Thank you, Martijn, for being my fantastic travel companion from 2003 to 2020. We have been such a great team together, both on the road and in other aspects of life. Although our roads in life diverged to other directions, I am happy you have still been an active part of this book as the first reviewer. There is no one who could review the travel tips, stories, and adventures better than you can. The passion for road trip travelling in Europe is something that we will share forever.

Thank you, Rainier, for accompanying me on all our life travels since the end of 2020. In a short period of time, we have shared a lot of adventures together, including the big move from the Randstad to the beautiful forests of the Veluwe. Although it was challenging at times, combining the renovation of the house with work and writing this book at the same time, you managed to keep both our heads cool and gave me all the room for writing my second

book in the short time frame that I had. Whether we light the fireplace in the house, in the garden or in the middle of nowhere on the road in Europe, you radiate what really counts in life.

A couple of other people also contributed to the creation of this book. Thank you, Martin, Dirk, and Ed, for reviewing the early versions and providing honest feedback where necessary while sharing a walk, wine, or climb together. Thank you, Mama, for sharing many places that you have discovered in Europe throughout the years. Some of them, like Stora Sjöfallet in Lapland and Ordesa Valley deep inside the Pyrenees, have made it to this book thanks to you and Papa. I hope the two of you will enjoy many more years on the road in Europe.

Thanks Paul and Susan, for collaborating again with me on this second book. I am proud on this tangible result we achieved together!

Lastly, thank you, Alex. With your wagging tail and unbridled enthusiasm for exploration and retrieving branches in the woods, you make me laugh every day. From classy hotel lobbies to dirty mud pools and crowded shopping streets, you somehow know how to deal with every situation and have stolen the hearts of many in the 17 countries that you have travelled to so far. You are a joyful travel companion, both on the road in Europe and in daily life.

Countless tunnels on the M18, Montenegro
43°13'60.0"N 18°50'43.2"E

Near Kyle of Lochalsh, Scotland, UK
57°17'38.8"N 5°37'50.9"W

Dubrovnik from Srd, Croatia
42°38'55.4"N 18°06'43.9"E

Meteora, Greece
39°43'15.7"N 21°38'01.4"E

Credits

Uitgeverij Terra is part of Uitgeverij TerraLannoo bv
P.O. Box 23202
1100 DS Amsterdam – The Netherlands
info@terralannoo.nl
terra-publishing.com

terrapublishing
terrapublishing

Text & photography
Sabine de Milliano – knalblauw.nl

Graphic design cover & inside
Susan de Loor – kantoordeloor.nl

First print – 2024

ISBN 978 90 8989 977 4
NUR 512 – 653

Photo cover
Trollstigen, Norway
62°27'18.2"N 7°40'20.2"E

Photo cover back
Near Ano Gliata, Greece
37°20'01.2"N 21°57'49.8"E

Photo front endpaper
Loch Tarff, Scotland, UK
57°09'10.7"N 4°35'41.4"W

Photo back endpaper
R335 near Cregganbaun, Ireland
53°40'51.1"N 9°47'28.0"W

Map projection
ETRS89-extended – LCC Europe
(EPSG:3034)